A PEACE OFFERING

ANDREW TEVINGTON
JD, MDiv

FULL CIRCLE PRESS
OKLAHOMA CITY

Book, text and jacket designed by Carl Brune

ISBN 0-9661460-3-4

Published by Full Circle Press
a division of Full Circle Bookstore LLC
1900 North West Expressway,
Oklahoma City, Oklahoma 73116

DEDICATION

I dedicate this book to my wife, Mary. Her support has been vital to my ministry, as well as to this writing. Her own faith has strengthened mine.

Thanksgiving

Many thanks must go to Jim Tolbert, owner of Full Circle Press and Full Circle Bookstore in Oklahoma City. He was the one who thought these newspaper columns might make a helpful book. I thank him for his support and his willingness to bring the message of tolerance and reconciliation to a wider audience.

The staff of *The Daily Oklahoman,* especially Ed Kelley, editor, and Carla Hinton, religion editor, have given me a regular forum to offer these reflections on America's growing number of faith traditions. I thank them for allowing me the opportunity to make an offering for peace.

Thanks must also be expressed to the editors of the manuscript, Pam Fleischaker, who helped with the big picture, and Shauna Struby, who I was privileged to meet for the first time as she performed the line editing. Thanks also go to the strictest and most honest editor on this project, my wife, Mary Everest Tevington.

Carl Brune designed the book, and I appreciate his creativity and hard work.

And many thanks to all the readers of the "Our Faiths" column; my patient faith teachers over the years, including my parents, William and Liese-Lotte Tevington; and my congregation—especially the extraordinary members of the Church of the Servant Chapel Community and adult Sunday School classes who were my guinea pigs as I strove to find understandable ways to explain complex faith issues.

Announcements

A few housekeeping issues: It is not appropriate to impose Christian calendar conventions in a book that discusses different religions. It also would be confusing to employ each faith tradition's own calendar system. For example, outside of Islam, few people have a grasp of when the year 1 A.H. was. *A.H.* is an abbreviation for "after *Hijra*." *Hijra* refers to Mohammed's flight from Mecca to Medina, which serves as the starting point for the Muslim calendar. In the prevalent Western calendar, 1 A.H. is the year A.D. 622. Many readers likewise would not know the civil year 2007 is in parts of the years 5767 and 5768, according to the Hebrew calendar, which traditionally was viewed as counting from the day of creation.

Since *A.D.* means *"anno Domini,"* referring to the "year of our Lord," Jesus Christ, the *A.D.* is not appropriate when talking about Judaism, Islam, or other religions outside Christianity. Keeping with current practice in the study of the world's religions, this book uses Western calendar numbers with *B.C.E.*, meaning "before the common era," for the period commonly denoted "before Christ," and *C.E.*, meaning "common era," for the time usually labeled as after Christ's birth.

A normal newspaper column should be 600–1,000 words. I break that rule virtually every time "Our Faiths" appears, and I thank the *Oklahoman* for looking the other way. Nonetheless, newspapers are limited by space considerations, and the column had to confine itself as necessary. I have taken the occasional liberty in this book of returning some material previously sacrificed to fit the news hole. In a few places, I deleted items of purely local interest, such as how many Quaker meeting houses there are in Oklahoma. I also corrected glaring spelling errors and any other problems appearing in the original publication. Many of the entries did not previously appear in the newspaper, but I wanted to include them for a fuller understanding of faith traditions in the United States.

Finally, each person develops his own religious practice within the structure of a communal faith. This book presents that communal faith, but within that tradition individuals pick and choose tenets and add or subtract practices for themselves.

Table of Contents

Say not, "I have found the path of the soul."
Say rather, "I have met the soul walking upon my path."
For the soul walks upon all paths.

— Kahlil Gibran

PRELUDE

As a statement of purpose, I chose to start with the answer to an angry response aroused by one of my newspaper columns about Islam. The e-mail I received was considerably longer than the question copied here and included the statement, "We have in our Bill of Rights No. 1 to be allowed freedom of our religion. We should demand that the Muslim religion—Islam—be eliminated in our country." It is an oxymoron that still bewilders me.

Q. You wrote about Islam like it was a true religion. Islam is a vile religion. Muslims are intent on destroying us. Do you have the courage to speak out about this?

— BEULAH

A. Differences in religion have been the excuse for war, holocaust, murder, and lesser mistreatment of people for millennia. Certainly we see this in world history, but we experience it in our own time as well.

Look to the recent past of Northern Ireland and the ethnic cleansing attempted in the former Yugoslavia. Witness the killings and enslavements still occurring in Sudan. Remember Ku Klux Klan cross burnings. Watch television news of suicide bombers in Iraq and the Holy Land. Recall September 11, 2001.

In part, ignorance causes this violence. Christians, Muslims, Jews, Hindus, Buddhists, Baha'is, and others do not know what one another believes, but they think they do. Even within Christendom, believers bear animosity toward one another because they don't know the true beliefs of other faith traditions.

Not so long ago, Americans seriously questioned whether a Roman Catholic could be United States president, and as a Mormon is touted for the 2008 presidential campaign, many decry his chances solely because of his faith.

I write believing that if adherents of various faiths understand one another, we will remove some of the ignorance leading to wars of words, battles with guns, and hostilities fought with food relief. It is a naïve belief, but God demands peacemaking in my small corner of the world.

Therefore, I will not attack any faith tradition in these pages. While I hold a strong faith, I will not proselytize in this space. I will not require followers of any tradition to be truer to their beliefs than I see adherents of my own Christian faith being to theirs.

I will, however, endeavor to set forth clearly and concisely the tenets of faiths across our nation and around the world in the hope we will truly see our brothers and sisters and peace will reign.

Every two weeks, my adopted hometown newspaper, *The Daily Oklahoman* in Oklahoma City, graciously allows me to use part of its news space for a ministry. It's a ministry that does not seek to convert anyone to my religious faith; instead, it aims to convert ignorance and suspicion into understanding and some measure of trust by explaining what people of various faiths believe.

By providing this space, the *Oklahoman* and now Full Circle Press give me an opportunity to make a peace offering to my community, state, country, and world at a time when the cold war of religious ideas often sparks into an inferno.

There is a war against religion in America, and it is being fought mostly by soldiers of faith, religion against religion. I offer this book in an attempt to bring peace to the battlefield through understanding.

Most of us hold our religious convictions because of three accidents: our geography, our family, and our culture. If I had been born in Pune, India, to a family with the last name of Patel, rather than on New York's Manhattan Island to an Irish father and German-Italian mother, I would probably be Hindu and have an affinity for the goddess Chaturshrungi, reigning deity of that western Indian metropolis.

Few of us pick our religion, though in America we might travel from one Protestant denomination within Christianity to another. Although it is not a tenet of my own Christian denomination, I believe God comes to us through each of the world's faiths. The Deity I understand does not discriminate because of accidents of geography, family, and culture.

As a Christian, I find support for this view in Paul's letter to the church in Rome, in which he explains, "all Israel will be saved" despite the fact Jews are not Christians, Romans 11:26. Paul's message in that chapter is simply worry about your own salvation and let God be concerned with everyone else's.

In my greater Christian community, I find the faithful do not believe Paul. They point to the Gospel of John to support their contention that all people who are not Christian are damned. That John 14:6 quotes Jesus Christ as saying, "No one comes to the Father except through me" does not shake my belief that God is available universally.

John's Gospel cannot mean only those who know the human Jesus may be saved, because then all people who lived before 6 to 4 B.C.E. and all who lived after 24 to 33 C.E., bracketing the period when Jesus walked the earth, are lost. Christianity teaches Jesus was both human and divine. John's prelude reports the divine Christ, known as "the Word," existed before time, and it is a major New Testament precept the divine Christ will exist for eternity. It is this Divinity that brings individuals to the Creator.

Many of us, whether Christian, Muslim, Jewish, or any other religion, attempt to limit God's abilities. We cannot. The passage in John's Gospel does not limit God acting as the divine Christ.

As I understand Jesus Christ, the Word, the uncreated Son of God, he has always been at work saving humanity and will always be about that same mission. Abraham and Moses were saved through the divine Son even though they did not know the physical Messiah, and the same divine Son saves me although I cannot know the human Jesus. The divine Son will save others, regardless of what name is applied.

When considering this issue, I recall the story of Sojourner Truth, a slave in New York State, when slavery was still practiced. In her autobiography, she reported she often went to a forest clearing and climbed on top of a large rock where she spoke with someone—she wasn't sure who—who responded to her over the years with help and advice. After Sojourner was freed, she attended church for the first time, and on hearing the sermon and prayers she discovered whom she had been conversing with all that time: Jesus Christ. It did not matter Sojourner had not known Jesus' name.

In the same way, it does not matter whether adherents of other religious traditions know Jesus' name. God can and does save them as God chooses. The judgment of their ultimate fate is not mine to make, nor yours.

The great Hindu peacemaker Mohandas K. Gandhi recognized this reality when he said, "I believe in the fundamental truth of all great religions of the world. I believe that they are all God-given and I believe that they were necessary for the people to whom these religions were revealed. And I believe that if only we could all of us read the scriptures of the different faiths from the standpoints of the followers of these faiths, we should find that they were at bottom all one and were all helpful to one another."

This book brings together a series of "Our Faiths" columns in hope of expanding knowledge about our neighbors who happen to express their beliefs in a different way than we do. Perhaps as importantly, the column and book seek to explain what our neighbors don't believe or do.

As a child I was reared Roman Catholic and was amazed to hear from some of my Protestant friends about the babies nuns were killing in the basement of our church. How could anyone who knew me believe such a horrible thing about my faith? Heck, we didn't even have a basement.

As readers have asked questions since the beginning of the "Our Faiths" column, it is clear America talks about many basements that aren't there.

Before we begin, you should know about my own biases. Since they are biases, I don't always recognize them, so let me just tell you quickly about my religious journey so you can spot the prejudices for yourself.

My father, a career American Army soldier, is Roman Catholic, specifically Irish Catholic, and my mother was Lutheran during her childhood in Germany before and during World War II. She converted at marriage. I was reared, as noted above, as a Roman Catholic and announced after my First Holy Communion at eight years old I would become a priest, but keeping with the prevalent mood of the 1960s during which I was a teenager, I became dissatisfied with the church and decided to look for something else. That journey took me first to Pentecostal meetings in Odessa, Texas—quite a contrast. Eventually, I sampled Baptist, Presbyterian, Episcopalian, and a myriad of other Christian denominations.

With international college friends in Stillwater, Oklahoma, I took part in Jewish, Muslim, Hindu, and Buddhist worship and study. I toyed with atheism but decided that at most, (or at least, depending on your view) I was an agnostic.

More comfortable with something closer to my cultural background, I returned to Christianity and settled into the United Methodist Church in a Washington, D.C., suburb and then Oklahoma because of the Methodists' free-will theology, hopeful preaching, and openness to religious expression within a basic framework of doctrine. There, I experienced God's call to representative ministry.

I attended Phillips Theological Seminary, a Christian Church (Disciples of Christ) school, while continuing to practice law. Today, I serve as a part-time local pastor in the United Methodist Church of the Servant in Oklahoma City, where I preach weekly in our early-morning Chapel service, while also acting as a full-time assistant district attorney for Oklahoma County.

From Atheists

My atheist friends are apt to see religion as a crutch for the weak. To them, religion provides individuals who are afraid to face life in all its reality with an excuse for failure, a security blanket for difficult times, and "magical thinking" to substitute for planning and hard work. For many atheists, religion is also, as Karl Marx put it, "opium for the masses." They view faith as a way the elite keep the majority population subdued. This question started an extended correspondence with a self-proclaimed atheist.

Q. Without having met you, I can tell you immediately that your brain and the ability to think for yourself were hijacked when you were about five years old. The hijackingwas done by your parents or their preacher.

There is no evidence of a god. No, none. The existence of the universe and of life is evidence [only] that a universe and life exists.

If you believe in the Bible, then you completely disagree with geology, anthropology, paleontology, biology, mathematics, astronomy, and common sense. To believe God is the author of the Bible is ludicrous. You need only to read the Bible to find inconsistencies, contradictions, falsehoods, injustices, misquotes, ill-conceived comments, misinterpretations, false prophecies, non-quotes, and ignored teachings.

—Jim

A. Atheists tend to be literal readers of the Bible or any other scripture they peruse. Religions' ancient scribes would be surprised to see such a limited parsing of the words they put to papyrus or parchment.

Before the twentieth century, the world's civilizations did not intend for their writings to be understood in a purely literal sense. For example, author Mason Weems's 1809 story of George Washington chopping down a cherry tree is not literally true, but that tale told school children about the first president's integrity in a memorable way. The "facts" were not true, but the message was.

Even today, we intend many of our writings to be understood beyond literal, printed words. Take an everyday example: On interstate highways passing through many cities, signs state the minimum speed is forty miles an hour. Only a reader who insists on reading the sign literally would claim a driver breaks the law by traveling twenty miles an hour during a wintry rush hour when a deluge of sleet pours down and ice covers the road.

Yes, in a literal sense, the Bible seems to contradict science. The favorite target for those attacking the Bible comes from a literal reading of the first chapter of the Book of Genesis. This is the famous story of God creating the world in six days.

And yes, the order of creation—light, plants, animals, people—is different in this story than in the second chapter of the same book. The second chapter is the beginning of the Adam-and-Eve story, where creation occurs in another order—man, plants, animals, woman.

There are many lessons taught in each of these stories, and certainly the concept that God created the universe is present in both. But the first creation story is more concerned with an entirely different lesson. That scripture wants people to understand the importance of Sabbath. The tale tells readers they need to rest at least once a week. A purely literal reading of the scripture misses this point.

The second creation story is also more concerned with a lesson other than where everything comes from. It wants people to understand the primary role of marriage in human society. Again, a purely literal reading misses the point.

That the ancient editors of the Bible put these two chapters together also provides a lesson missed if a reader does not delve beyond a word-by-word approach. In effect those editors say, "Look, there are differences. Don't miss them. Don't ignore them. Ponder why we did that."

The reason the Bible includes two seemingly contradictory stories at its very beginning is to make the point this book requires a lot of work on the reader's part. Anyone who wants to understand may not simply stay on the page's surface, looking at ink squiggles. The reader seeking knowledge must read for the deeper meaning.

My experience as a pastor has shown literal readers of scripture are most often either fundamentalists or atheists. Fundamentalists take the "God said it, I believe it, that ends it" approach whenever inconsistencies arise; while atheists want to throw everything out the window any time an irregularity crops up. I confess I am not a literal reader of the Bible or any other scripture. This question came in an e-mail the day the preceding column was published.

Q. What a shock to read you consider atheists to be the people who interpret the Bible literally. I guess Christians pick and choose what is fact or fiction in the Bible. It might help them make sense of the incongruous Bible, but who decides what is fact and what is fiction? You? Your denomination? The Pope? Who?

— Cheryl

A. We must be careful with what we read. I said atheists tend to be literal "readers" of scripture. I did not say they interpret the Bible literally. Atheists tend not to interpret it at all.

The Bible itself directs how it is read. It's not a question of fact or fiction. Instead, the questions are, what lesson is taught and through which literary form?

The Bible contains many different forms of literature and not all are read in the same manner. For example, the historical accounts of First and Second Kings are not approached the same way as the poetry of Psalms. Poetry most often uses non-literal imagery, while history rarely does. To read both the same way is an error.

Some passages contain prayers of misguided people, such as the exile's desire to "dash" infants against rocks in Psalm 137:9, which cannot be understood as God's word. Other parts contain literal direction for life, such as the prohibition against false testimony in Exodus 20:16. These may not be read the same way.

The broad spectrum of Christianity has many approaches to biblical interpretation. Fundamentalists who grew out of the Niagara Bible Conference of the late nineteenth century believe the Bible is inerrant.

They tend to read scripture literally and have the greatest conflict with the theories of evolution and the big bang.

Even among many fundamentalists, however, the difference among types of scriptural literature is used to understand the words' meaning. Many fundamentalists do not understand the Gospels' parables as true stories. Instead these short stories are instructional devices Jesus used to make a point.

The point of Luke's Gospel parable about the woman searching for a lost coin is not that someone actually swept her home fastidiously. The point is God perseveres in saving those who are lost.

Other Christian groups approach their study of the Bible in less literal ways than their fundamentalist cohorts. While the battle cry of many sixteenth-century European reformers was *sola scriptura*, meaning "scripture alone," the majority of so-called mainline Protestant denominations join their Roman Catholic and Eastern Orthodox companions in applying tradition and reason to Bible reading.

These groups do not believe today's world is the sole possessor of intelligence and spiritual guidance. Individuals from the past had tremendous insight about God and the Bible too. The writings of Thomas Aquinas, Augustine, Jerome, and others, as well as the meticulously drafted statements of early church councils provide a tradition Bible readers may employ to help understand scripture.

These denominations also apply reason to what they read. Believers from this group can accept evolution, for example, and biblical accounts of creation. Using reason, they acknowledge geology's statement about Earth's ancient age and biology's accounting of the epochs during which life evolved. Using that same reason, they recognize an apparent conflict with the Book of Genesis.

But with an open, reasonable mind, they are not relegated to the either/or answer that one must be right and one must be wrong. These readers recognize the problem lies not in scripture or science, but in the reader's understanding of the two. In Genesis, the message is not about *how* God created the universe, and in geology and biology, science makes no attempt to explain God.

For readers applying reason, Earth is ancient and life progressed over eons. At the same time, for them, God created today's universe in that ancient past and over those eons. These readers do not see Genesis as a how-to manual for creating the universe; instead, it is guidebook to relations between God and people and to living with one another under God's tutelage.

For Christians following the teachings of John Wesley, including Methodists and many Pentecostals, it is vital to apply another factor to biblical interpretation. The reader's experience with the Holy Spirit—some may call this God's new revelation, given personally to the reader—is equally important.

Jim, the atheist I wrote about earlier, is a persistent reader and arguer. Regardless of whether Jim ever agrees with me, I'm glad he writes because his correspondence provides the opportunity to explain basic principles.

Q. Predestination is all through the Bible. It seems to me if the Bible is the word of God, then God has already made up his mind who will be saved and who won't be saved. Therefore, all prayer and all preaching are in vain. Looks like you might get an honest job that produces something for society.

—Jim

A. Don't confuse pleading with prayer.

Intercessory prayer—a request for God to intervene in human events—is not the sole form of prayer. But even intercessory prayer is not primarily about the request, and among the faithful it is never about begging.

As explained in an earlier column, the Christian doctrine of predestination deals with the afterlife and an understanding of whether God elects only certain individuals to obtain eternal life in a heavenly existence. Predestination is not concerned with this current, physical life.

Intercessory prayer seeks blessings for this life: healing of a sick relative, food for a hungry family, safe return of a soldier posted to Iraq. These requests have nothing to do with a person's ultimate salvation. Outcomes for such things are rarely predetermined.

That said, the purpose of intercessory prayer is not limited to making a Christmas gift list. The first of many purposes for intercessory prayer is for the believer to acknowledge God's existence. The second is to recognize no matter what happens, the petitioner trusts God's decision. The third purpose is to give therapeutic voice to pain, sorrow, or anxiety. The fourth is to make the request. The fifth purpose is to listen for the "still, small voice" granting the requests, or explaining a different and better approach that may be taken, or indicating why the request should not be granted, or uncovering the true and inappropriate motivation for asking. Begging has no part here because such pleading makes the prayer about us rather than about God and because it obscures the divine message.

The strictest doctrine of predestination was taught by John Calvin. Despite his belief each person's salvation or lack of salvation had been decided by God, Calvin wrote in *The Institutes of Religion* prayer remains important because each Christian "knows it to be his duty to lay his desires before God, lest his faith should become drowsy or torpid." As Calvin saw it, the doctrine of predestination does not make prayer vain any more than reaching the age of majority makes calling your mother on Mother's Day or her birthday a useless act.

Calvin recognized other forms of prayer in addition to intercessory prayer. Invocative prayer reminds believers of God's presence and their love for the Supreme Being. It gives voice to that affection, just as we tell our mothers we love them. We have a fondness for our mothers despite the fact that when we become adults they no longer do all things for us. In the same way, we love God regardless of what predestination might teach.

Confessing prayer causes us to be honest with ourselves. Confession might be seen as a vain act because God is supposed to already know what we have done. But confession is for the believer's good rather than for God's. By confessing and owning the sin, we take the first step toward personal improvement and repairing our relationship with God.

Prayers of thanksgiving rise from individuals who see they have worked through a difficulty with God's help. Believers also give thanks for those things so many of us today take as mundane—food on the table, clothes to protect us from the sun, shelter from the rain.

"Thank you" is more than a social nicety; it is recognition of an effort put forward on our behalf. Saying it will not obtain us anything more because the work is finished, but those two words tell the person who receives it, "I acknowledge your value and your exertion on my behalf."

This column repeats the previous question, but changes the subject to preaching.

Q. Predestination is all through the Bible. It seems to me that if the Bible is the word of God, then God has already made up his mind who will be saved and who won't be saved. Therefore, all prayer and all preaching are in vain. Looks like you might get an honest job that produces something for society.

—JIM

A. I have responded to the comment about prayer. Now, let's deal with preaching.

Among the changes Martin Luther instituted when he ignited the Continental Reformation was placing tremendous emphasis on preaching rather than ritual. In the Roman Catholic Church which Luther came from, the most important part of the Mass was celebration of the Sacrament of the Eucharist, or Holy Communion.

Receiving the sacraments, including regular Holy Communion, was seen then and continues to be seen now in the Catholic and Orthodox churches as a means of obtaining God's grace. But Luther believed, as he wrote in "The Freedom of a Christian," that grace was received through faith and faith "is produced and preserved in us by preaching why Christ came, what he brought and bestowed, [and] what benefit it is to us to accept him."

Luther understood the great benefit of faith was our ultimate salvation, but he also recognized faithful living brought order to a chaotic world and morality to a sinful people. In a 1528 sermon, Luther taught human beings made progress toward a humane society only when they learned and obeyed the Ten Commandments and other admonitions from God.

Even earlier than Luther, synagogue-attending Jews recognized preaching as a way of teaching adherents about God's Law. Synagogues began as a means of preserving Jewish faith during the Babylonian Exile half a millennium before the birth of Jesus. When the Romans destroyed the rebuilt Jerusalem Temple in 70 C.E., Jews lost the only place where Davidic Law allowed sacrifices. Synagogues, which had been secondary to the Temple, again became the focus of Jewish worship outside the home.

Philo of Alexandria, an ancient Jewish philosopher, said synagogue sermons quenched "a thirst for refreshing discourse" and instructed listeners "in what is best and what is most conducive to their welfare . . . by which their whole life may be made better."

Likewise, during Friday noon prayers, Muslims attending their mosques hear a sermon called the *khutbah*, which is a "remembrance of God," in keeping with instruction from Surah 62:9 in the Qur'an. In part the *khutbah* remembers God by explaining how faithful believers should live so the world will be a better place.

Over the years, Catholic and Orthodox churches, while still placing major emphasis on the Eucharist, have increased the importance of what is normally called the homily, another name for sermon, though usually shorter than Protestant sermons.

In all these traditions, the sermon has developed not only to teach about God but also to pass on, as the Catholic Catechism puts it, the "deposit of Christian moral teaching . . . a deposit composed of a characteristic body of rules, commandments, and virtues proceeding from faith . . . and animated by charity."

A proper sermon brings its hearers faith and also exhorts them to look at their lives and the practices of our society. The speech holds up a mirror and says, "Let's look at ourselves. What can we do to make this world a better place now and to improve ourselves today?" The sermon is as interested in the here and now as it is in the hereafter.

Our mosques, churches, temples, and synagogues are the only places in today's American culture where questions of ethics, right-and-wrong, and life's principles are discussed regularly. Without sermons, many Americans would not be confronted with the problems of our age and asked to remedy them. Lacking a weekly call to a higher moral purpose, we may find no reason to improve our society, so long as we have our own comforts. Absent homilies, most of us would not have to face questions about what we do and why we do it.

As Socrates said, "An unexamined life is not worth living." Sermons, homilies, and *khutbahs* put our lives under the microscope.

On Islam

This is the first question-and-answer set appear in "Our Faiths." Frank is a member of a Sunday school class I asked to give me questions to start the column. Because of September 11, 2001, the war on terrorism, and the conflict in Iraq, most of the class wanted to know about Islam. Along with needing to thank my Muslim friends from college, I am indebted to my Islam professor in seminary, Dr. Rabiatu Ammah, a Ghanaian woman and devout Muslim, who brought some order to my fragmented knowledge about Islam.

Q. With all that's going on in the world, it seems we should know about Islam. What are this religion's basic beliefs?

— FRANK

A. It's impossible to summarize any faith's beliefs in a single newspaper column, but our understanding of Islam can begin by looking at the Five Pillars of Islam. These pillars identify the foundational practices of Islam's two major forms: Sunni and Shia.

The first is the *Shahadah,* which is a confessional statement uttered by believers: "There is no God but God, and Mohammed is His prophet."

The *Shahadah* recites Islam's monotheism and declares whom Muslims look to for instruction about God and God's way. In Islam, God revealed the scripture, known as the Qur'an through Mohammed. (The holy book's name is also transliterated *Koran,* but *Qur'an* has become the preferred spelling.)

The second pillar of basic Muslim practice consists of five daily prayers, known as *salat.* This pillar obliges every Muslim to pray before sunrise, at noon, during the afternoon, at sunset, and during the night. These five times of prayer are a minimum.

Each prayer follows a set liturgy of words and body positions, such as lying prostrate, kneeling, bowing, and standing. After reciting the liturgical prayers, believers are free to add other prayers.

In preparation for prayer time, believers must make themselves and the area where they pray acceptable to God. For the person, this is done through ablutions, which involve washing various parts of the body, including the hands, feet, mouth, ears, and private parts. The prayer area is made acceptable by cleaning it and laying down a prayer rug.

The third pillar is the *zakat*. This practice is somewhat similar to Jewish and Christian tithing. The *zakat* requires every adult Muslim to give two-and-one-half percent of his excess wealth for charity each year. Certain rules define excess wealth. A Muslim may give the *zakat* to a mosque, organized charities, or directly to people in need.

The fourth pillar is fasting during the Islamic calendar month of Ramadan. This month-long fast is often called the *saum,* which simply means "fasting."

From dawn to dusk each day during Ramadan Muslims take no food or drink and don't smoke or engage in sexual activity. Believers add a group of twenty liturgical prayers to their regular nightly prayer and spend time in reflection. Ramadan ends with the Night of Power, which marks the occasion about fifteen hundred years ago when God started to reveal the Qur'an to Mohammed.

Because Islam uses a pure lunar calendar, the month of Ramadan moves within the Western civil calendar. Over a twelve-year period, Ramadan will occur during part of each of the Western calendar's months. The appropriate greeting during this time is "*mubarak* Ramadan," which means "blessings of Ramadan."

The fifth pillar is the pilgrimage known as the *Hajj*. Every physically and financially able Muslim is expected to travel to Mecca, the seat of Islam, at least once in her lifetime. *Hajj* activities take place over ten days in the twelfth month of the Muslim calendar.

While in Mecca, Muslims engage in prayer and numerous rituals that—to the surprise of many—do not relate directly to Mohammed. The emphasis obviously is on God, but also on Abraham, prophet for three of the world's great religions.

Bill is a member of a different Sunday school class at my church. The Sunday after the first column on Islam was printed, a number of my congregants wanted to discuss Islam. This was one of their questions.

Q. You wrote that the fundamental practices of Islam's two major forms, Sunni and Shia, are the same. If that's the case, what makes them different?

—Bill

A. Shi'ite and Sunni Muslims arose as separate groups shortly after Mohammed died in 632 C.E.

Muslims who would later be called Shi'ites believed the only proper successor to Mohammed, who had no sons, was his cousin and son-in-law Ali. But other believers who would become known as Sunnis said any male member of Mohammed's tribe who was pious, politically astute, and well-educated in the ways of Islam could be successor or *caliph*. Living in a patriarchal culture, the Arab Muslims did not consider Mohammed's daughters appropriate successors.

The Sunnis carried the day, saying Ali was too young and inexperienced to be caliph. After the deaths of other caliphs, Ali was named the leader of the Islamic people, but his caliphate was short-lived. He was deposed and eventually killed.

The name Shi'ite comes from the Arabic *shiah i-Ali,* which means "the partisans of Ali." The name Sunni comes from *Sunnah,* which is the second-most important text in Islam. While the Qur'an consists of God's revelations to Mohammed, the *Sunnah* consists of Mohammed's sayings and deeds, serving as examples to believers.

While Sunnis and Shi'ites share many beliefs and practices, there are differences. The major difference comes in the Shi'ite belief in the infallibility of the *Imamate*, which is the group of leaders Shi'ites accepted after Mohammed's death instead of the Sunni caliphate. Each *imam*, or leader, was a descendent of Mohammed. These imams' religious teachings are considered perfect.

Within Shi'ism, believers disagree over who was an imam. One group accepts twelve imams, another says there were seven, and another claims only five. The "Twelvers" or "Imamites" believe the last imam, Mohammed al-Mahdi, did not die but withdrew from earthly life in 873 C.E., in what is called the Great Occultation. Twelvers await the return of this hidden imam.

"Fivers" reject the hidden imam and continue to elect imams from direct descendants of Ali as the need arises. While other Shi'ites do not accept the first three caliphs, Fivers do and have the closest relationship with Sunnis.

"Seveners" do not accept Mohammed al-Mahdi as the hidden imam but await the return of Ismail, the imam who died in 760 C.E. Neither the Twelvers nor the Fivers accept Ismail as an imam.

All three Shi'ite sects accept Hussein ibn Ali, the grandson of Ali, as an imam. The caliph's Sunni troops massacred Hussein and his followers while the Shi'ite group was traveling to Iraq.

The massacre took place on Ashura, the day dedicated to celebrating God's creation of the universe and Noah's exit from the ark following the Great Flood. Today, Shi'ites commemorate Ashura as a day of mourning. For Sunnis, the day remains a celebration of creation, but its observance is optional.

The Internet has ignited a revolution in communication and knowledge. Unfortunately, some of the material on the World Wide Web is false and sometimes malicious. This writer forwarded an e-mail that sought to justify the war in Iraq.

Q. I received an e-mail that said many things about Iraq and the United States and ended by quoting a verse from the Koran: "For it is written that a son of Arabia would awaken a fearsome Eagle. The wrath of the Eagle would be felt throughout the lands of Allah and lo, while some of the people trembled in despair still more rejoiced; for the wrath of the Eagle cleansed the lands of Allah; and there was peace, Koran 9:11." The e-mail said the son of Arabia is Saddam Hussein and the eagle is America. Is this true?

— Frank

A. The e-mail you included in your correspondence is a piece of misinformation on par with the work of Nazi propagandist Joseph Goebbels, as it attempts to contrive support for the Iraq war from "the other side's" scripture.

Whether the war is correct or not, no one can be allowed to concoct false scriptural teachings—from the Qur'an or the Bible or any other holy book. The Qur'an, also transliterated as *Koran,* is the scripture of Islam. Like the Bible, the Qur'an is divided into chapters. In the Bible, the chapter numbers start over again when a new book starts. In the Qur'an, the chapter numbers are consecutive from the beginning to the end of the entire scripture.

The Qur'an has one hundred fourteen chapters, called *surahs.* Each surah is divided into verses. If we go to the eleventh verse of the ninth surah, as the e-mail cites the alleged passage, we find a scripture bearing no resemblance to the quoted material. It does not mention eagles, sons of Arabia, or any of the other things mentioned in the e-mail.

Surah 9:11 comes after the Qur'an directs Muslims to take in idolaters so these so-called sinners can learn about God and be saved. The verse says, "But if they repent, establish regular prayers and pay *zakat,* they are your brethren in faith: Thus do We explain the signs in detail for those who understand." (*Zakat* is similar to the Jewish and Christian tithe.) This translation is provided in the English-language Qur'an the Kingdom of Saudi Arabia makes available as part of its mission to spread Islam.

A more easily understood translation of the Qur'an was written by N.J. Dawood in London. He translates the verse this way, "If they repent and take to prayer and render the alms levy, they shall become your brothers in faith. Thus do We make plain Our revelations to men of knowledge."

Christians have developed concordances listing all words used in the Bible and telling where each occurrence is in scripture. Muslims have done the same for the Qur'an.

A review of *A Concordance of the Qur'an,* published by the University of California Press, shows no use of the words *eagle, hawk, vulture,* or anything similar anywhere in the Qur'an, so the misrepresentation is not a matter of the e-mail author simply getting the citation wrong.

The closest the Qur'an comes to mentioning such a bird is in Surah 5:4, which states, "They ask you what is lawful for them [to eat]. Say: 'All wholesome things are lawful for you, as well as that which you have taught the birds and beasts of prey to catch, training them as God has taught you.'"

These are not words justifying either side in the Iraq war.

This e-mailed question included an attachment claiming to explain why Muslims are fundamentally different from Americans—as though there are no Muslim Americans. The answer provoked a huge response. While many Christians attacked the column for "apologizing" for Islam, others wrote with thanks for providing a better understanding of the religion. Muslims expressed astonishment that any Christian would write anything positive about Islam. Dr. Imad Enchassi, imam for an Islamic center in Oklahoma City, asked me to lunch with some of his community. While I was hoping to bring understanding to the non-Muslim population, I discovered this group, which felt harassed, began to believe there might be hope for peaceful coexistence.

Q. My Bible study leader said he had looked and found the Koran never mentions the word *love.* I could not find it either.

— Cary

A. We always have to be careful where we get our information about different faith traditions. Sometimes the source has a desire to favor his religion over another.

For example, a number of authors have written about religions other than Protestant Christianity for the sole purpose of helping evangelists to convert practitioners of different faiths to a certain denomination within Christianity. While such writers believe they are doing God's work, their description of another faith is suspect. At other times, the source simply doesn't have adequate knowledge.

The claim that the word *love* doesn't appear in the Qur'an is untrue. That word or some version of it, such as *loving,* appears more than one hundred times in the Muslim scripture. Other words that in context are synonyms for *love* also appear often in the Qur'an.

The scripture discusses God's love of human beings, as when the

Islamic book teaches, "Allah loves the equitable," Surah 5:42. (A *surah* is a chapter in the Qur'an.) The Qur'an also says, "Surely Allah loves the god-fearing," Surah 9:4.

As might be expected, the Qur'an teaches that God provides for love between husband and wife, as stated in Surah 30:21, "He creates for you mates out of your own kind so that you might incline towards them, and He engenders love and tenderness between you: in this, behold, there are messages indeed for people who think!"

In Islam, words alone are insufficient to show faith. A person must also act as urged by Surah 19:96, "Those who believe and do good deeds, for them the Beneficent will surely bring about love."

In Surah 3:92, Muslims learn, "You cannot attain to righteousness unless you spend out of what you love. And what you spend, Allah surely knows it."

Following this teaching, the Qur'an calls on believers to practice charity. For example, in Surah 90:12-20, Muslims are exhorted to free the slave, feed the hungry, care for the dying, and show mercy to others. Driving the point home, Surah 3:148 says, "Allah loves the doers of good to others."

The claim the word *love* is absent from the Muslim holy book is typically made in an attempt to prove Islam is a religion preaching intolerance and practicing hatred. This is a view supported by those whose only knowledge of Islam is the fact Islamist terrorists contend they are adherents of the Muslim faith.

Some members of my own national ancestry also claimed to have been implementing true Catholic or Protestant teachings in Northern Ireland's terrorist nightmare, but no serious Christian would mistake those actions for Christian love. People of all faiths do well to remember examples from their own history when looking at one another.

The Qur'an does indeed teach love among people. "True piety does not consist in turning your faces towards the east or the west, but truly pious is he who believes in God, and the Last Day; and the angels, and revelation, and the prophets; and spends his substance—however much he himself may cherish it—upon his near of kin, and the orphans, and the needy, and the wayfarer, and the beggars, and for the freeing of human beings from bondage," Surah 2:177.

Beulah's first e-mail opened the prelude in this book. No doubt, there are Muslims attempting to justify first-strike war by referring to their religion, but such justifications are based on false teachings. We see from what is happening in the world Islam has many of the same problems we have witnessed in Christianity, as the Bible has been used for the same violent purposes.

Q. Andrew Tevington, on February 24, gives from the Qur'an the surahs concerning love. I would like for him also to give the quotations having to do with the commands for the Muslims, if they want a place in paradise with all those virgins, to kill all the infidels, the Christians, etc., those who will not convert to Islam.

— Beulah

A. The vast majority of Muslims recognize three basic sources of written religious instruction: the Qur'an, Islam's holy book; the *Sunnah*, which explains the Qur'an through the way the Prophet Mohammed lived; and the various *hadith* which offer further explanation of the Qur'an.

Neither the Qur'an nor the *Sunnah* contains a promise of virgins in paradise for killing anyone. There are many volumes of *hadith* writings. Those available to me do not contain such a promise, either. No orthodox Muslim source reports the existence of such a passage.

The Qur'an does contain verses about killing and war, as do the Hebrew Bible and Christian Bible. When looking at these verses, a reader must always keep the passage's context in mind.

For example in the Hebrew Bible, or what Christians call the Old Testament, God commands, "Whoever sacrifices to any god but the Lord must be put to death under solemn ban," Exodus 22:20.

Neither Jews nor Christians today take this law literally when dealing with peoples of other faiths, especially since the next verse orders, "You must not wrong or oppress an alien; you were yourselves aliens in Egypt," Exodus 22:21.

Similarly in the Christian New Testament, Jesus is quoted as saying, "You must not think that I have come to bring peace to the earth; I have not come to bring peace, but a sword," Matthew 10:34. Christians understand the *sword* in this verse as a symbol of the social and personal change that comes to a new believer, rather than as a weapon of physical war.

In the same Gospel, the Beatitudes teach, "Blessed are the peacemakers; they shall be called God's children," Matthew 5:9. Christ is understood as the "Prince of Peace."

The Qur'an says, "And kill them wherever you find them, and drive them out from where they drove you out, and persecution is worse than slaughter," Surah 2:191. (*Surah* means chapter). Without careful reading, this verse can be alarming. It is important to note that these actions are a response to Muslims being driven from their homes.

Looking at the context further, a reader discovers this verse tells Muslims what to do when a conqueror attempts to prevent them from observing their religious ways, "They will not cease fighting you until they turn you back from your religion, if they can," Surah 2:217.

The Qur'an teaches the battle should continue only until the opponent allows Muslims to again practice their religion freely. "Fight them until there is no persecution, and religion is only for Allah. But if they desist, then there should be no hostility except against the oppressors," Surah 2:193.

The Qur'an does not teach conversion "at the point of a sword" as many of us were taught in elementary school studies of the Crusades. "There is no compulsion in religion—the right way is indeed clearly distinct from error." [Surah 2:256].

For a Muslim, forced conversion is no conversion at all. A person must come to Islam through her own choice.

Both the Qur'an and the *Sunnah* provide for peaceful coexistence with people of other faiths. "The Messenger of Allah said, 'One who kills a non-Muslim person under protection will not even smell the fragrance of Paradise,'" Sunnah, Al-Awsat.

A Muslim may befriend non-Muslims and live in peace with them, "Allah forbids you not respecting those who fight you not for religion, nor drive you forth from your homes, that you show them kindness and deal with them justly. Surely Allah loves the doers of justice," Surah 60:8.

Gordon wrote a very long and thoughtful e-mail about trying to understand Islam from his Christian point of view. His question about Jesus in the Qur'an shows how carefully we must read any scripture.

Q. The Qur'an seems to teach that Jesus was not crucified, but had a likeness crucified in his place, Surah 4:157.

The Qur'an makes numerous references to Jesus as a prophet, an apostle of God. It would seem the Muslims do respect and honor Jesus as a prophet, an apostle of God, even though the Qur'an seems to indicate that He pulled a major deception, and, if this were true, He should be regarded as a liar and a deceiver.

How should I reconcile this? If the Muslims believe that Jesus was a liar and a deceiver, yet still worthy of honor as a prophet and an apostle, should I conclude that being a liar and a deceiver is entirely acceptable, and even honorable, in the Muslim society?

— Gordon

A. You are correct in understanding that Islam honors Jesus Christ as a prophet. The Qur'an teaches Jesus was born to a virgin, probably in Bethlehem, but under a palm tree rather than in a stable, as Christians understand.

Muslim scripture also says Jesus was sent by God to profess the true faith to a world that had corrupted the Lord's message brought by previous prophets, including Noah, Abraham, and David. The Qur'an refers to Jesus as the Messiah, meaning the anointed one, and teaches God specially chose him for a ministry emphasizing peace, kindness, and compassion.

Islam also recognizes Jesus' many miracles of healing the sick, raising the dead, and feeding the multitudes with a few pieces of fish and bread. In addition, the Qur'an teaches Jesus performed miracles not found in the Bible, such as crafting birds out of clay and bringing them to life—although a version of this miracle story is found in the Infancy Gospel of Thomas, believed by some to have been written by Gnostic Christians.

Muslims also wait for Christ's Second Coming. This return is not mentioned in the Qur'an but is taught in various other Islamic writings known as the *hadith,* including a statement by Abu Hurairah, a companion of Mohammed, who writes, "I swear by God, Jesus son of Mary will come down, a just king; he will kill the swine, and break the cross, and remove the poll-tax from the unenfranchised; and camels will not be rode in his time on account of the immensity of wealth, and man's being in want of nothing; and verily enmity, hatred and malice will go from man," *Mishkatu'l-Masqabih,* Book 23, Chapter 6.

The Qur'an, however, draws a line at the Christian teaching about Christ's divinity. Islam finds this Christian teaching unacceptable, believing the Deity cannot be contained within so small a package as a human being. Muslim scripture says Jesus is merely an example of God's divine power and quotes the Lord as saying about Jesus, "He was naught but a servant on whom We bestowed favor and We made him an example for the Children of Israel," Surah 43:59.

Christians insist Jesus was and is the only Son of God, "true God from true God," as the Nicene Creed puts it. It is a debate that will not be settled by human means.

The quranic verse you cite refers to Jesus and says, "[T]hey killed him not, nor did they cause his death on the cross, but he was made to appear to them as such." This teaching is at odds with the Christian Gospels which state that Jesus was crucified and died, as reported, for example, at the New Testament's Mark 15:37.

The Qur'an, however, does not say that Jesus deceived anyone. Maulana Muhammad Ali, one of the last century's translators of the Qur'an into English, wrote Islam believes Jesus was nailed to the cross and suffered.

When Jesus cried out, "My God, my God why have you forsaken me?" as reported in the biblical Matthew 27:45, the Lord heard the prayer and caused Jesus to appear dead while saving his life through miraculous means, according to Ali. Other Islamic scholars write that God, acting out of love for Jesus, exchanged Judas Iscariot, Christ's betrayer; Simon of Cyrene, who carried the Messiah's cross; or another person for Christ.

Islam does not consider Jesus a liar and deceiver. Nor does it regard those who offer falsehoods as worthy or honorable. As much as Christianity, Judaism, and the other widely practiced religions of the world, Islam considers truth a virtue.

On Native American Religions

In Oklahoma, Native Americans comprise a large percentage of the state's population because of its history as Indian Territory. Most Oklahoma Native Americans today are Christians; in fact, the first official white settlers were met by Cherokee Christian missionaries who offered help. Interest in Native American traditions remains high.

Q. I was told Indians starting using peyote in their religion after they came to Oklahoma. Is this true?

—No Name Given

A. American Indians' use of peyote did not begin in Oklahoma, but the Sooner State was the site of the first official church to administer the hallucinogen in its religious rites. Oklahoma also gave birth to new religious practices involving peyote.

Peyote is a spineless cactus containing a fuzzy growth resembling a caterpillar. This growth is known as the peyote button and contains a mind-altering chemical. Its use in Indian religious ceremonies was first recorded by Spanish missionaries in Mexico shortly after Hernando Cortez conquered the Aztecs in 1521, but archaeological evidence suggests the cactus button has been part of some native Mexicans' worship for about ten thousand years.

Peyote grows on both sides of the Rio Grande. American Indians from what is today southern Texas joined compatriots from northern Mexico in employing the drug for their sacred rituals. From the southern Texas peoples, peyote use spread to nearby groups of Apaches, Comanches, Kiowas, and Tonkawas. In the 1830s, when the U.S. Government began forcing these nations to relocate to Indian Territory (present-day Oklahoma), the tribes brought peyote with them, although sometimes calling it by different names, including the Comanche *wokowi* and Kiowa *se-nay*.

Not all Native American nations include peyote in their religious observances. Even among groups in which some adherents use peyote, many other tribal members do not. *Peyote Religion* is the name given ritual practices using the cactus to differentiate those traditions from other tribal religious customs. While some native religious practices are unique to specific Indian nations, Peyote Religion has stretched across tribal lines.

Early on, the American government fought against Peyote Religion, following precedent set by the Spanish Inquisition in the 1600s, when it declared peyote use a "superstition" and "heresy" and banned the drug throughout the Spanish Empire. In 1914, in an attempt to secure First Amendment protection for their religious practices, Oklahoma peyote religionists hired lawyer Henry S. Johnston, who would later become the state's governor. Johnston drafted papers to incorporate the First Born Church of Christ. Its members combined Peyote Religion and Christianity in their services. Because tribes were recognized as nations rather than churches, the First Born Church of Christ appears to be the earliest official church to include peyote in its ritual.

In 1918, another group of Oklahomans incorporated the Native American Church, which also practiced a combination of Peyote Religion and Christianity. While the First Born Church of Christ disappeared, the Native American Church remains and has spread throughout the American Southwest, West Coast, and Great Plains, as well as into Canada.

The peyote ritual brought to Oklahoma is known as the Half-Moon Ceremony, named after its crescent-shaped altar. Following relocation, Caddo Tribe member John Wilson introduced the Big Moon Ceremony, which he said God revealed to him. Later, the Cross Fire Ritual developed, apparently outside Oklahoma.

Despite common belief, adherents do not use peyote to create visions, and it is never taken when a believer is alone. It is administered in an all-night group ceremony as a sacrament believed to heal, assist prayer, enable prophecy, and locate lost objects or people.

The ceremony is led by a roadman or road chief, named after the symbolic road drawn on the altar where a peyote button is placed during the service. Among nonbelievers, the most famous roadman was Quannah

Parker, a principal Comanche chief in Oklahoma after relocation. The roadman is assisted by a drummer, who provides a rhythmic beat during various parts of the ritual, and a cedarman, who tends the fire and provides smoke for ritual cleansing at different times in the ceremony.

The participants sing, pray, and tell stories from dusk to midnight. Then the roadman blesses water, which each worshipper drinks. After drinking, adherents consume peyote buttons, and the group resumes singing and praying until dawn, when a ceremonial meal of corn, fruit, meat, and water is taken. The ceremony ends after the roadman preaches and a final song is sung.

Bible readings, tobacco smoking, and other native traditions are included to a greater or lesser extent throughout the service, depending on the form of Peyote Religion practiced. The older Half-Moon Ceremony includes tobacco and a lesser emphasis on the Bible. The Oklahoma-born Big Moon Ceremony eschews tobacco and includes more Bible reading. The newer Cross Fire Ritual adds even more Bible lessons.

Under fairly new federal law, many artifacts collected from Native Americans nations must be returned to their rightful owners. I don't know whether authentic Kachina dolls fall into that category, but this e-mailed question provided an opportunity to explain little-known religious beliefs.

Q. My grandfather collected a handful of Kachina dolls that I have inherited and want to display. Since these dolls are religious objects, is there a special way I should display them?

—No Name Given

A. *Kachina* is a term in the Hopi language referring to the spirits who bring rain in the arid Southwest, where various peoples live who were given the name *Pueblo* by Spanish explorers. The term is also used to refer to the group's village, originally constructed of adobe.

While each Pueblo clan or village recognizes these spirits, they do not all use the same name for these ethereal beings. For example, the Tewa people of north central New Mexico call them *okhua.* In American society, however, the term *kachina* has come to mean the rain-bringing spirits venerated by any of the Pueblo peoples.

In the Pueblo religions, kachinas are mostly benevolent spirits who visited the villages every year to bring rain so crops could grow and feed the people. After a while, the spirits taught selected villagers rituals and dances to perform to bring rain. The spirits directed their protégés to enact the special events at certain times each year. Kachinas then stopped visiting the villages.

The protégés created kachina societies to carry on the spirits' activities and to pass the information they learned from generation to generation. The most well-known of these activities are the dances the societies perform publicly. The dancers—who are all men, even though they may represent female kachinas—believe they disappear as individuals during a properly conducted dance and become filled with the spirit they portray.

The dances are preceded by private ceremonies in the village *kiva*. A kiva is a partially buried religious chamber covered with an adobe roof. The exact nature of the ceremonies varies from pueblo to pueblo. The ceremony may last only one day or more than two weeks, and its ritual secrets are reserved for members.

In preparation for the rituals and dances, kachina societies teach new members how to appear in the form of the spirits. Each dancer wears a particular mask, draws on certain body paint images, and dons special clothing and accessories to represent one particular kachina.

In an effort to teach children about the kachinas, the societies carve what the outside world calls kachina dolls. Originally, each doll was crafted as the exact replica of a particular kachina, and the child given the doll was told about the spirit and its characteristics.

It was important for the children to know the spirits so the young could show proper respect required to ensure rainfall. According to Pueblo belief, f respect is not shown, kachinas may withhold rain for the year. It was also important for the children to recognize the handful of demon kachinas intent on bringing trouble to the Pueblo village or the child's clan.

Many of the kachina societies were offended by the sale of authentic kachina dolls to tourists. These sales were seen as disrespectful to the spirits. In the twentieth century, many villages began creating kachina dolls that do not represent any of the two hundred fifty or so spirits honored by the Pueblo peoples. These dolls are produced for the tourist market demanding artifacts. Kachina societies believe this production protects the respect required of kachinas. Other individuals in the Pueblo see the work as a way to make money.

If your grandfather obtained actual kachina dolls, you may want to display them as the Pueblo people do. Pueblo families hang the dolls on walls or from roof rafters in their homes. The dolls are not mixed with everyday knick-knacks, but are given a place where they may be studied so the spirit will be recognized in the future.

At the same time, it is important to recognize kachina dolls are not worshipped as idols. Even the kachina spirits themselves are not worshipped, but are only honored in Pueblo society.

I was privileged to attend a wedding that included Christian and Native American spiritual elements. Before the service, I had an informative conversation with the shaman who performed the blessing of the wedding space and couple. What I learned came in handy for this question.

Q. Why do Indian religious ceremonies involve so much smoking?

— Eric

A. Smoke has been an important part of Native American, traditional African and other long-established religious rituals for many centuries.

In Native American tradition tobacco was brought north from the South American continent long before the arrival of Columbus in the New World. It was and continues to be used as a gift for important individuals and as a ceremonial necessity.

Tobacco smoke and other smoke are seen as means of communicating with the spirits. Just as in "high church" Christianity, smoke is a symbol of a person's prayers rising to God. This use is reminiscent of God-pleasing smoke rising to the heavens from Noah's burnt offerings in Genesis 8:21 or the Israelite priests' fiery sacrifice in Exodus 29:41.

Tobacco is understood to be the food of spirits in many Native American cultures. Converting it to smoke allows spirits to partake of the plant and creates a bond between the spirit and physical worlds. That bond is seen as vital to curing illness and restoring balance to the physical world.

Smoking tobacco is performed as a group ceremony, often as a means of welcoming strangers or other individuals the tribe wants to have good relations with. In many ways it can be understood in the same way as ceremonial meals in European and Asian cultures, in which sharing food is a peacemaking process.

In Native American practice, tobacco is rarely used by itself but is often mixed with other plants, usually depending on the ceremony's purpose. Smoke from various types of plants is also used to bless people and things. Steve Old Coyote, a shaman of Cree heritage living on the Fort Madison Reservation among the Suquamish people of northwest Washington, recently explained to me different types of smoke are believed to provide distinct blessings.

For example, smoke from burning sage is used to remove negative energy from a place and individuals. Smoldering cedar provides smoke to prevent the negativity from returning. Sweet grass aromas protect the shaman performing the ritual cleansing from becoming contaminated by the forces being removed.

On Judaism

In the past ten years or so it seems there has been a tremendous surge in interest among Christians about all things Jewish. Some nationally produced Bible studies have emphasized Christianity's Judaic foundation; perhaps that explains why Martha, a Christian, asked this question.

Q. What is Yom Kippur?

—Martha

A. *Yom Kippur* is a Hebrew term meaning "Day of Atonement." It is the holiest of Jewish holidays and is sometimes called the Sabbath of Sabbaths, as each Sabbath is considered the holiest day on the Jewish calendar.

Yom Kippur is the climax of ten days of penitence at the Jewish New Year called *Rosh Hashanah,* meaning "head of the year." Judaism operates on a lunar calendar with modifications to keep the seasons within the same months each year. Under this calendar, Rosh Hashanah occurs during parts of the Western calendar's September and October.

On Yom Kippur a faithful Jew recognizes he has sought to repent for sins and has attempted to truly change to ways more pleasing to God, but the penitent individual also recognizes his repentance is incomplete. An observant Jew knows that acting alone he will continue to fall short of the perfection sought, so the repentant worshipper asks for God's forgiveness and assistance.

Using a play on words from the English name for the day, rabbis say a believer seeks "at-one-ment" with God.

In ancient days Yom Kippur included the use of a scapegoat, as reported in Leviticus 16. A priest symbolically tied the sins of the people to a goat using a ribbon and sent the animal away into the wilderness. This activity does not continue today.

Yom Kippur today is structured around five services at the synagogue. In addition to attending this full day of prayer, scripture reading, and ritual, each believer is expected to forgive those who have given offense and to seek forgiveness from individuals the believer has offended. Traditional Jews also mark the day by following the five restrictions or afflictions: no eating or drinking, no bathing, no anointing of the body, no wearing of leather shoes, and no sexual relations.

This question came in a conversation with a woman who was concerned she had not shown proper respect to the family of a deceased friend. It is these Rituals like these, surrounding events experienced by everyone may lead us to a fuller understanding of one another.

Q. A Jewish friend of mine died, and his funeral was the next day, before I could make arrangements to attend. Why do Jews hold their funerals so quickly, and how can I offer my condolences at this late date?

—Lenora

A. Judaism considers a family's duty to bury its dead a sacred obligation set forth as one of the 613 commandments in Hebrew scripture.

In Deuteronomy 23:21, Torah teaches the body of an executed criminal must be buried the same day as the execution. While there is no similar scriptural direction for non-criminals, Jewish authority has understood this teaching to require speedy burial of all deceased people.

The tradition of quick interment also arises from a desire to avoid defilement of the body, to protect the community's health, and perhaps most importantly, to help grieving family members to begin finding their way to healing. The swiftness of burial, however, does not prevent you from offering your condolences and other support. Following the funeral, the family returns home and "sits *shivah.*" *Shivah* means "seven" in Hebrew. The surviving family remains at home for seven days of intense mourning.

This is a good time to show your support. If you do visit, keep in mind while family and friends are welcomed to the home, the bereaved are not required to greet them, as survivors are allowed to mourn and given license to forgo the normal duties of hospitality.

In keeping with Jewish tradition, do not initiate conversation with the surviving family. Leave it to survivors to start conversation if they choose. In all religions good friends are always concerned about what to say at this time. It is appropriate to tell mourners sitting *shivah,* "I wish you a long life" or "You should have no more pain." More important than what visitors say is listening to family members. Even though survivors may not speak to visitors, the consoler's presence is considered a great *mitzvah,* a religious act of kindness.

The tradition in many American communities, regardless of religion, is to bring a prepared dish for the family so they won't have to concern themselves with cooking. If you choose to do this, remember kosher requirements. Traditional Jews don't eat pork or shellfish, and they don't combine dairy products—including cheese—with meat. If you are unfamiliar with Jewish dietary law, it is best to take a vegetable dish.

Many friends want to help the bereaved by taking them on outings. This is not appropriate during *shivah.* After *shivah,* the family may want to leave the house; however, for traditional Jews, any outing including music, whether on the radio, live, or otherwise, is inappropriate for thirty days following burial. This month is known as *shloshim.*

Even after this month, traditional Jews avoid concerts, movies, and other occasions perceived as joyous until eleven months have elapsed from the date of the loved one's death. Friends should be present during this time but must remember these special restrictions.

During the eleven-month period, a special prayer known as the *Kaddish* is said at set intervals by the survivors. If the deceased was a parent, the *Kaddish* is recited every day.

Also during this time, most Jewish families erect a tombstone at the gravesite. In the United States a special unveiling of the marker is typically conducted. Here is an opportunity to support the family with your presence. Some Jews believe the tombstone should be put up during *shloshim;* others say it may be erected at any time in the first year after death.

Mourning never ends in Judaism—or for that matter, in any religion—but it becomes less intense after the initial eleven months. Family members are expected to fully integrate themselves into society again. While the loved one will never be forgotten and the loss will never be completely overcome, Judaism does not find it healthy for survivors to remain isolated after this period.

However, in recognition of the importance of the deceased loved one to the family, the *Kaddish* is recited again each year on the anniversary of the death. This anniversary is known as the *Yahrzeit.* Those who support the survivors will offer a word of remembrance on the *Yahrzeit.*

Talking about "keeping kosher" raises the perfect opportunity to note every person practices religion differently—even within the same faith tradition. While Orthodox Jews may keep kosher down to the last phrase of law, many Reform Jews see no need to be bound by the rules. They take more of the biblical prophets' approach: It's more important what is in your heart than how closely you follow the letter of the law.

Q. We had a party and invited some new friends who are Jewish. Knowing they don't eat pork, I was careful not to include any on the buffet table. We had beef and shrimp, but I was embarrassed to discover Jewish people do not eat shellfish. I understand about trichinosis in pork, but why do they not eat shellfish?

—Janet

A. Jews, Hindus, Muslims, Mormons, Seventh-day Adventists, and members of many other faith traditions follow dietary laws prohibiting eating or drinking various foods and beverages.

In Judaism permitted foods are called *kosher.* The word simply means "fit." Prohibited foods are known as *trefah.* When talking about food, *trefah* today means "forbidden" but comes from a Hebrew word which referred to a wild beast tearing meat from an animal. The Bible teaches during their desert wanderings the Israelites were told by God, "You are to be my holy people. So do not eat the meat of an animal torn by wild beasts. . . ," Exodus 22:31.

This law is one of many detailing foods that may not be consumed. At Leviticus 11:9–10, Moses passed down a law believed to be from God which says, "Of all the creatures living in the water of the seas and the streams, you may eat any that have fins and scales. But all creatures in the seas or streams that do not have fins and scales . . . you are to detest."

Shrimp and other shellfish do not have fins or scales; therefore, they are *trefah*.

A common belief among adherents of religions and denominations choosing not to follow dietary laws is the thought food bans are based on health considerations. If pork contains trichina roundworm larvae, undercooking the meat will fail to kill the parasite, leading to illness. Upon this discovery, many people automatically assumed God issued the food laws to protect health.

However, trichinosis can also be contracted from eating undercooked wild game not prohibited by the Hebrew Bible. In various faith traditions, food laws may have a salutary effect on health, but this is not the reason the prohibitions were instituted.

The first food law recorded in the Bible is God's admonition to Adam not to eat fruit from the tree of the knowledge of good and evil. Although the story includes a warning that eating the fruit will doom Adam—and all humankind—to eventual death, the law is not presented to protect Adam's physical health. The fruit serves as a constant sign of God's presence in Adam's (and later Eve's) life. The universal consequence of Adam and Eve consuming the fruit serves as a continuous reminder to the human family that disobeying God's law has a price.

In the tale of the Great Flood, after Noah and his family leave the ark, the Bible teaches God bans only one food, "meat that has its lifeblood still in it," Genesis 9:4. Again, the law serves to remind Noah and his family of God's presence on a daily basis. Jews also interpret this and other laws regarding meat as showing the importance of life of all types. An animal must be humanely killed and prepared because God gives value to each created life.

In the Exodus account of the Israelites' escape from Egypt, more food laws are given, such as the prohibition against eating leavened bread around Passover. This law reminds Jews of their heritage and of God's providence.

The greatest volume of commandments concerning food is found in the Book of Leviticus. The laws are given to assure Israelites remain clean, meaning holy or set apart for God.

These laws concerning potential foods Jews see every day remind the faithful they belong to God. The commands also tell Jews they have the special purpose of being an example to the world, as mentioned in Deuteronomy 4:6.

Jews do not keep kosher to save their health; they keep kosher to say, "Every day, I remember that God is my creator, my leader, my provider and my protector. I will honor God by following his commandments and performing the acts he requests of me."

Adventism—the belief the "end of the world" is upon us—is as popular today as it was a century ago or nearly two millennia ago when Apostle-to-the-Gentiles Paul was preaching. For Christians, Adventism is about the Second Coming of Christ. For Jews, it is about the coming of the Messianic Age. This question came from a Christian.

Q. I was told by a person very knowledgeable about the Bible the end of the world will come when the Jews in Israel find a pure red calf and that they are looking for one and almost had it recently. Where can I find this scripture?

—Ed

A. You won't find a biblical passage stating the discovery of a red calf will signal the beginning of "the end times."

In the Book of Numbers, God informed Moses how to purify individuals who came in contact with dead bodies. A "red heifer without defect or blemish" was to be sacrificed and its ashes mixed with water. Small amounts of this "water of purification" were then sprinkled on anyone who touched a dead body. It was also used to purify any tent where a person had died, Numbers 19.

No one coming in contact with a corpse was allowed to worship in the wandering Israelites' tent Tabernacle or the stone Temple settled Jews later built in Jerusalem until she was purified with this potion. The mixture was saved for generations because a pure red heifer was and is extremely rare. According to Jewish sources, only eight or nine were known from Moses' time to 70 C.E., when the second Jerusalem Temple was destroyed by the Romans—a span of at least thirteen hundred years and perhaps longer.

The rest of the Bible is silent about purification with this mixture, but the Mishnah Tractate Parah and other oral Jewish tradition deal with the issue in more depth. *Mishnah* is a Hebrew word meaning teaching. The Mishnah is a digest of Jewish oral law compiled in the second century C.E.

A party of Orthodox Jews and a group of conservative Christians believe another red heifer is needed to create a new batch of the water of purification so the Third Temple can be built on Jerusalem's Temple Mount. Currently, only a foundation wall of the former Temple remains, a remnant known as the "Wailing Wall."

This small group of Orthodox Jews, following Mishnah and other traditions, want to rebuild the Temple so the Hebrews' sacrificial worship of God can be reinstituted. Not all Jews agree with the concept. Many Jews reject the call for a new Jerusalem Temple, agreeing with Moses Maimonides, twelfth century Jewish philosopher and rabbi, who said God replaced sacrifice with prayer. Some within the Jewish community believe reconstruction of the temple will herald the Messianic Age—the coming of God's anointed person, who will restore the Hebrew nation to its proper place and bring peace to the globe.

The Christian group, relying on readings of Matthew 24, Hebrews 13:12-13 and the non-canonical Epistle of Barnabas 7:1-8, believes the rebuilding of the Temple and its purification will signal the Second Coming of Christ. This group includes some Christian ranchers in the United States who are attempting to breed a pure red heifer.

Not all Christians agree Christ's Second Coming requires constructing a new temple. The New Testament Book of Revelation teaches the great battle of good and evil that will bring about the end of the world as we know it will follow the Second Coming. It is usually better to refer to this anticipated event as the "end of the era," rather than the "end of the world" because Revelation teaches that the world will continue to exist but with a new sense of righteousness.

More than one question came because of celebrity actions in the entertainment and political worlds.

Q. Madonna and other celebrities have taken to wearing red-string bracelets as part of something called Kabbalah. Is Kabbalah some new movie-star religion? And what's the red string for?

—Mary

A. The easiest part of your question is about the bracelet. The red string forming it comes from a much longer piece of string wound around the Tomb of Rachel, one of the biblical matriarchs. The tomb is located in the Middle East's West Bank between Jerusalem and Bethlehem.

The string is wrapped about the tomb as certain prayers are said. Because of the matronly love Rachel exhibited in the Book of Genesis, the bracelets are thought to ward off the power of the "evil eye."

The evil eye is a gaze by someone envious of another person's good luck, great wealth, or outstanding status. It is a look lasting too long, according to Celtic tradition, although the concept is found in virtually all ancient societies. The covetous stare is thought to bring bad fortune to individuals receiving it, causing them to lose success and prosperity. Despite the term *evil,* the look is thought to be given by people who are good and honest but are momentarily overcome by jealousy. The general goodness of the person giving the look makes it hard to guard against the evil eye and its repercussions.

Kabbalah is a form of Jewish mysticism and is not new. Various threads of mystic thought came together about seven hundred fifty years ago in Provence, France, to form Kabbalah. These mystic practices quickly moved into Spain, where kabbalists published *Sefer ha-Zohar,* meaning "the Book of Radiance." Today the book is known as the *Holy Zohar,* or simply *Zohar.* It serves, with the Hebrew Bible, as the canon for Kabbalah.

Mysticism generally is a way of understanding the universe involving direct personal experience more than traditional theological study. Some writers refer to mysticism as knowledge by acquaintance rather than knowledge by description. Many Jewish, Muslim, Hindu, and Christian mystics attempt to know the Divine more fully by uniting with God through meditation.

Taking their cue from the first chapter of Genesis, in which God begins the creation of the universe simply by saying, "Let there be light," kabbalists believe God brought all things into being through the twenty-two letters of the Hebrew alphabet. That alphabet was also used to compose the Hebrew Bible; therefore, kabbalists teach the hidden meaning of the letters in the Bible, especially the Torah, reveals God more fully than conventional reading.

In Hebrew, letters also serve as numbers. Kabbalah finds ten divine numerical entities or *sefirot* through the alphabet. These ten entities are not separate gods but aspects and manifestations of the one God. In some ways, they may be analogous to the three divine persons of the Christian Trinity.

The first of the ten sefirot is Nothingness from which God comes. The next two are Wisdom and Understanding through which God creates the rest of the universe, including the remaining *sefirot.*

The first two created *sefirot* are Love and Power. Love contains God's free-flowing grace and mercy, and Power contains God's judgment and limitations on humanity. These two must remain in balance because any listing in one direction or the other creates evil, as kabbalists understand it.

Out of properly balanced Love and Power comes the sixth sefirot, Beauty, which is the part of God we may visualize. The seventh and eighth are Splendor and Eternity. Together, they provide prophecy, God's way of directing and correcting humankind. The ninth sefirot is Foundation, which is the procreative force of the universe.

The final sefirot is Presence, referring to God's availability to us. For a kabbalist, Presence and Beauty are the focus of religious life. These aspects of God are what they meditate on to achieve a fuller relationship with God. As with most theistic mystics, the personal relationship with God is the kabbalist's foremost goal.

Because Kabbalah is difficult to understand and challenges many long-held religious beliefs, teachers of the mystic practice generally limit students to married people with previous religious training, who are more than forty years old and exhibit emotional stability and high moral standards.

On Christianity's Shared Issues

During my undergraduate years, two of my Muslim friends shared the name Iqbal, Syed Iqbal Ali and Syed Iqbal Haider. They told me it's not a common name in their Pakistani culture. When I received an e-mail from another Muslim by the same name, I was taken back to those days of learning about Islam and celebrating Eid al Adha. Iqbal's question goes to the heart of Christian understanding about God.

Q. Kindly answer a question of a Muslim. Christians say they are monotheist, yet they worship three gods. Can you justify it? The Prophet Mohammed, peace be upon him, taught there is one God.

—IQBAL

A. This question and its answer draw one of the major dividing lines between Christians on one side and Jews, Muslims, and other monotheists—believers in one God only—on the other.

The Christian doctrine of the Trinity teaches there is only one God who exists in three persons. This doctrine can be discussed, but it can never be completely explained. Since ancient times, church leaders have said the Trinity can be understood fully by God alone, while it remains a mystery to theologians and everyday practitioners of Christianity

Perhaps it is best to go back to Latin, one of the languages in which this mystery was discussed in some of the early church councils. Latin referred to each of the three aspects of God as a *persona,* the same word that gives us our term *person.* In Latin, a *persona* was a mask worn by an actor. These masks are familiar to us today as the happy and sad faces drawn on theater programs.

Because an early actor often played more than one role on stage, the mask identified for the audience which character was performing. As the drama progressed, an actor might go back and forth among two, three, or more different personas.

One mask might be the male hero, another could indicate a woman, and a third *persona* might represent a villain. In each case, the actor was the same, but the characters or roles were different. Thus, the parts were played by the same actor, but none of the characters were the same.

The Trinity, consisting of the Creator, Jesus Christ the Son, and the Holy Spirit, is God. In our ancient stage play example, God is the underlying actor. The Creator is one mask, the Son is a second persona, and the Holy Spirit is the third.

Just as the male hero role in our play is not the woman character, the Creator is not the Son. However, just as the actor plays each part, God is each aspect of the Trinity.

As early theologians put it, God is the Creator, the Son, and the Holy Spirit, but the Creator is not the Son, the Son is not the Creator, the Son is not the Holy Spirit, the Spirit is not the Son, the Spirit is not the Creator, and so forth.

Another way to look at it is to consider the different roles each of us plays during the day. You might be a father, a doctor, and a soccer player. There are many things you do as a father you don't do as a doctor or a soccer player. Certainly, many of the functions you perform as a doctor, you do not perform as a soccer player or as a father. In fact, you behave somewhat differently in each of these three roles.

But you do not act completely differently, because your underlying personality guides you in each of the roles.

In Christianity God is the sole God, all-powerful, all-loving, and all-knowing. At the same time, Christ is the Savior and the expression of God's love. The Holy Spirit is counselor and the expression of God's continuing presence. The Creator is producer and the expression of God's beneficence.

There are a few New Testament-based churches and denominations that do not accept the doctrine of the Trinity. An example is the Jehovah's Witnesses. Jehovah's Witnesses agree the three persons exist but teach only the first, the Creator, is God. They understand Jesus as the "first creation" of God. They believe the Holy Spirit is a force sent to the world to intervene on God's behalf.

The Doctrine of Predestination is one of the most misunderstood in Christianity. Mark's question set off a flurry of inquiries about the issue. Some were discussed in the "From Atheists" section; others are dealt with below.

Q. How can Presbyterians believe that God predestines everything when there are so many evil people and events in the world? Surely God doesn't cause man to be evil.

—Mark

A. Outside reformed churches, which include the Presbyterian denominations, people often confuse the doctrines of predestination and predetermination.

The predestination doctrine comes in various forms. One teaches God has chosen a few people to realize salvation at the end of the current era. These individuals were elected by God even before they were knit in their mothers' wombs, to borrow a phrase from Psalm 139.

Another form of the doctrine teaches God has not specifically chosen individuals to be saved. Instead, because of omniscience, God simply knows who will accept the gift of grace leading to forgiveness and salvation.

A third form emphasizes human beings are unable to obtain salvation by themselves because of their inherently sinful nature. God has predestined assistance for humanity so individuals may overcome this nature in accepting God's grace.

For most members of the Presbyterian denomination, predestination is a "doctrine of comfort," which says believers need not worry because God has taken care of their ultimate end. The Presbyterian's current concern, then, is to engage in a loving life praising God. As a doctrine of comfort, predestination is concerned with the end times—the ultimate salvation of God's creation.

Predetermination, on the other hand, concerns itself with everyday events. The most extreme form of predetermination teaches nothing happens on earth unless God causes it to happen. If a hatchling falls out of a tree, God pushed it. If that fledgling teeters on the nest's edge and is saved from falling by a gust of wind toppling it back into the nest, God did the blowing.

In a more ominous example, if a tornado destroys your home, the extreme form of predetermination says God led the funnel to your doorstep. If the tornado wipes out the houses around you but spares you, God's hand blocked the wind's path.

The question of evil is a difficult one for believers in extreme predetermination because under this doctrine nothing occurs without God's active participation. To explain evil, extreme predetermination teaches Satan interferes with God's plans.

On the opposite end of the spectrum is Deism, which holds God created the universe but now watches life unfold without getting involved. For the Deist, God never intercedes, instead allowing the laws of physics, chemistry, and biology to play out unhindered. For the Deist, therefore, intercessory prayer is considered useless.

Most Christians find themselves somewhere in the middle of the predeterminist-Deist spectrum. On this middle ground, many Christians believe human free will and natural coincidence account for many events, but they may also understand divine intervention occurs as God sees fit.

Presbyterians and other reformed church denominations most often do not accept extreme predetermination. For these believers, everyday acts progress in various ways and for assorted reasons; however, most rest assured no matter how events unfold, their ultimate salvation is in God's hands.

Melody's question raises the major problem with predestination: How can it be fair for salvation to be decided even before we are born? One answer is Arminianism, which started out as a concept within Calvinism, although many Calvinists fought it when it was being developed. Today Arminianism has been combined with the Doctrine of Free Will to create a different view.

Q. As a Christian, the thought God already has chosen who will be saved and there is nothing I can do about it if he hasn't chosen me grieves me. Where is the justice and mercy God is supposed to show?

—Melody

A. The concept God has elected a few people to be saved and has chosen all the rest to be damned is part of the Calvinist doctrine known as "predestination absolute." It is not universally accepted by Christianity or endorsed in its entirety by all Calvinist churches.

A number of Christian denominations—especially those tracing their heritage to John Wesley's movement to revitalize the Church of England—teach the Arminian view, which sees God offering grace to the whole world.

In the late 1500s and early 1600s, Jacobus Arminius, a minister in the Dutch Reformed Church, began teaching John Calvin's doctrine of predestination absolute was contrary to Christ's purpose for taking human form and suffering crucifixion.

Calvin taught human beings are utterly depraved and unable to save themselves. Their only hope for salvation rested in God's grace, and God had elected just a few individuals throughout history to receive that grace.

Arminius agreed people are unable by themselves to overcome the power of sin. He also agreed that only by God's grace could believers be saved. But he taught Christ died so the sins of everyone could be forgiven, not just the sins of a few. God's grace, therefore, was available to every person.

The Dutch minister said a believer accepted God's grace by having faith

Jesus Christ was indeed the savior. The believer's salvation was contingent on retaining faith in Christ. If a person once believed but then rejected the faith, her salvation would be lost. Calvin, on the other hand, taught salvation could never be lost.

Eventually the doctrine of "open theism" was introduced by some churches as an addition to Arminianism. Open theism teaches God decided to allow each human being to have free will. Each person, therefore, has the independence to choose to accept God's grace or to reject it. Those who accept will be saved, those who reject will be damned. God does not predetermine the accepters or rejecters under this doctrine.

Acceptance of God's grace requires faith—a true belief, not just empty words. Many who espouse open theism believe the validity of a person's free choice is shown by his "fruits." In other words, if a person truly has faith and accepts God's grace, he will act like a person of faith. Those actions will include works of love for God's creation, including fellow human beings. This group finds support for its theology in the Epistle of James's statement, "[F]aith by itself, if it is not accompanied by action, is dead," James 2:17.

This reliance on acts as an expression of faith has led some opponents to accuse open theists and Arminians of abandoning Paul's teaching that salvation is by grace through faith alone. The open theists and Arminians deny they teach salvation through works. They insist they comport with the doctrine of salvation through grace by faith, but see action as a sign of true faith at work.

While the doctrine of predestination is recognized as a "doctrine of comfort," many Christians find greater comfort in Arminianism and free will.

I've discovered plenty of people will keep me on track as I write the column. If they believe a question hasn't been answered, they're not afraid to say so.

Q. You avoided the real question about predestination. He was really asking why God allows evil. The presence of evil is proof God does not exist.

—No Name Given

A. The existence of evil no more proves the non-existence of God than contracting a cold proves the non-existence of infection-fighting white blood cells in your body. Sighting a lion on the African savannah does not disprove the presence of a zebra. The snow of winter does not disprove the coming tulips of spring. The question regarding how an omnipotent, omniscient, omnibeneficent God can allow evil in the universe has befuddled theologians and ordinary believers for millennia.

It is the question at the heart of the Book of Job in the Hebrew Bible, known to Christians as the Old Testament. Job demands answers about troubles that have befallen him, and eventually learns there are some things about which humankind is ignorant and will remain so. "Surely I spoke of things I did not understand, things too wonderful for me to know," he says, Job 42:3b.

Many who consider the question of why wickedness exists agree with the teaching from the Qur'an that human beings choose to follow God or not, Surah 90:10. Those who opt not to devote themselves to God generate evil; therefore, malevolent forces are humanity's creations.

For the Buddhist life involves suffering, and evil is simply part of suffering. In a teaching reminiscent of Gnosticism which competed with Judaism and Christianity for the favor of the ancient Mediterranean world, Buddhism teaches the simple fact of physical existence brings pain. Only by becoming enlightened and thus freeing itself from the cycle of reincarnation will humanity escape the problem.

For the Mormon evil is the consequence of Adam and Eve's choice, and while the consequence is awful, it is not entirely bad. Faced now with the choice between good and evil, human beings "will prove them[selves] herewith, to see if they will do all things whatsoever the Lord their God shall command them. . . ," *Pearl of Great Price,* Abraham 3:25.

In the belief system of the Navajos and many other Native American religions, unpleasant and even terrible events unfold because the divinely created balance of the universe is knocked out of kilter by people's thoughts, actions, or failures to attend to the proper etiquette of life. Only through a cleansing ritual, may life be restored to balance.

Some theologians define evil as a moral issue and remove from consideration any natural act, such as floods or tornadoes. These events are neither good nor bad intrinsically. They simply occur as a result of the operation of physics. For this group evil then is completely a human choice and a result of the exercise of free will.

My understanding of evil arises from the awareness two things exist: God and the universe. God created the universe and when this happened the Deity did not recreate God—a second god. The Divine Being is complete and in that completeness, perfect. That perfection affirmatively means total goodness exists within God.

The universe is not complete since it is not God. This incompleteness means an aspect of God is missing in the creation, and this absence gives us evil, whether it is immorality on the part of humans or adverse natural events.

I don't know Carol, but she is the type of person I love to have in a Sunday school class or Bible study—she wants to know why. Her letter provided many columns. Her question on baptism required two columns.

Q. Can you explain why different churches baptize by dunking and others by sprinkling and why some baptize babies and others don't?

—Carol

A. Baptism is a practice predating the Christian church. As we know from the Gospels, John the Baptist, a Jew, baptized many people in the Jordan River, including Jesus. Other faith traditions of that day, such as the Eleusinian Mysteries cult headquartered in Eleusis outside of Athens, Greece, practiced a cleansing ritual in the Mediterranean Sea that ahs been called baptism. Hindus for centuries have dipped themselves in the Ganges River or poured water from the stream on themselves as part of a sin-cleansing ritual.

The major outward difference between these baptism practices and the Christian ritual is recitation of the words, "I baptize you in the name of the Father, and of the Son, and of the Holy Spirit" by Jesus' followers. The wording comes from Matthew 28:19, in which the resurrected Jesus gave his apostles the "Great Commission," directing followers to "go and make disciples of all nations, baptizing them in the name of the Father and of the Son and of the Holy Spirit." The term "baptize" comes from a similar-sounding Greek word which means "to dip, plunge, or immerse." It is also used to refer to fabric dyeing because cloth is plunged into liquid coloring agents.

Christians such as Baptists, Eastern Orthodox, and members of Churches of Christ insist on completely immersing the baptizee in water. For these adherents, the origin of the word clearly indicates proper baptism is accomplished by immersing or dunking, as you say, the individual.

(The term "Dunkers" was used pejoratively to refer to Schwarzenau Brethren, who immigrated to the United States from Germany in the 1800s. They are part of the Church of the Brethren today, and many take that once-derisive name proudly.)

Churches practicing immersion baptism point out the symbolism of the act whereby a person dies to his former life and is reborn into the family of Christ. Immersion signifies burial, and release from the water connotes birth. In fact, some ancient descriptions of the ritual indicate baptizees were held under water until they nearly ran out of breath to make the representation more vivid.

The immersion group points to Jesus' baptism in the Jordan River as additional proof that complete submersion is required. Within the immersion group, there is disagreement about how many times a person must be submerged. The Orthodox and Brethren require an individual to be immersed three times, once for "in the name of the Father," once for "and the Son," and again for "and the Holy Spirit." Most Baptist groups require only one plunging.

Churches practice two other forms of baptism. One is sprinkling, known officially as aspersion, and the other is pouring, known as affusion or infusion, depending on the group. Roman Catholics, Episcopalians, and Mennonites are among the groups that pour; while Presbyterians and Moravians are included in the groups that generally sprinkle.

Other groups, such as United Methodists, Reform Church in America, and United Church of Christ, use any of the three methods and perform baptism in the manner preferred by the baptizee or family.

The non-immersion groups say the baptism offered by John is not the new baptism offered by Jesus; therefore, what John did does not control how Christian baptism should be performed. Some who practice baptism by sprinkling or pouring agree baptize comes from the Greek for dipping or plunging, but say it also means "to wash." They point to Jesus washing his apostles' feet at the Last Supper as an indication other forms of the ritual could be possible. They argue the Bible does not show explicitly how Jesus thought baptism should be performed.

The pouring baptizers also rely on the earliest-known picture of baptism being performed. It is a mosaic from about 150 C.E., showing water being poured over the baptizees as they stand in an ankle-deep pool. This method conforms to archeological evidence obtained from the oldest-known ruins of a Christian church, found in present-day Iraq. The structure believed to be church's baptismal font is a pool with low walls that would not allow immersion. The pourers and sprinklers also say the important part of baptism is God's grace—his forgiveness for sins and free offer of salvation—and the amount of water used is irrelevant.

The difference in the forms of baptism arises mostly from the various churches views on whether the New Testament sets definite directions. Some find such direction and some don't.

This is the same question as above, but deals with the second part of Carol's question.

Q. Can you explain why different churches baptize by dunking and others by sprinkling and why some baptize babies and others don't?

—CAROL

A. Last time, we discussed how churches perform baptism—by immersion, pouring, or sprinkling. This time, let's look at the reasons for baptizing infants or just those individuals old enough to make a choice.

On a January evening in 1525, two men walked to the town square of Zollikon, Switzerland, where despite the cold, a fountain still poured out water. Each man baptized the other with the fountain's water and began the Anabaptist Reformation, which said infant baptism was ineffective.

Up to that time, most Christians were baptized as babies, regardless of whether they were members of the Eastern Orthodox or Roman Catholic churches or Martin Luther's new Evangelical Church or Ulrich Zwingli's newer Swiss Reformed Church.

"Anabaptist" means rebaptizer. Swiss reformers, using Zwingli's new translation of the Bible, said they did not find evidence in the Scripture that children were baptized in the earliest days of the church. They also believed Christians had to choose to accept God's grace, an act impossible for infants.

For Anabaptists, the phrase "saved by grace through faith," which was one of the rallying cries of the Continental Reformation, and meant a person had to express faith in Jesus Christ before baptism. That expression of faith was the method for accepting God's grace. Since babies could not express faith, Anabaptists believed all people baptized as children must be baptized again after expressing their faith.

Today's churches practicing only "believer's baptism" follow this Anabaptist theology. On the other hand, practitioners of infant baptism say grace is God's unearned gift. No one has to do anything to earn it, and in fact, cannot do anything to merit God's grace. God pours out grace on infants, just as God gives grace to adults.

Groups baptizing babies agree that at some point individuals baptized as children need to express their faith. Except in the Orthodox churches, the later expression is accomplished in what is called confirmation.

For some churches practicing infant baptism, the gift of God's grace is not a one-time event. Instead, it is seen as coming in three parts: prevenient grace, justifying grace, and sanctifying grace.

We can think of prevenient grace as the gift God gives at a person's birth so the child will look for God. This prevenient grace is sufficient for baptism, in the view of churches practicing infant baptism.

Justifying grace comes at the moment a person recognizes Christ's sacrifice is specifically for him. This often happens when a person recognizes he has committed a sin and does not deserve forgiveness. Unmerited forgiveness comes, then, only from God's love. Justifying grace is the full concept of grace recognized by many of the believer's baptism churches.

Sanctifying grace is God's continuing gift which raises love for the rest of humankind in the believer's heart. Through sanctifying grace, God and the believer work together to make the world a better place.

Practitioners of infant baptism point out the New Testament does not prohibit the ritual. They also find support for it in those biblical instances when a believer's entire household was baptized, such as with Lydia in Acts 16:15. They argue the household would have included children.

In the church world, we think everyone knows what we're talking about when we throw around terms, but meanings have changed over the years. Let's consider three of these terms.

Q. A friend and I were discussing our religions when I referred to her religion, Southern Baptist, as Protestant. She said Baptists aren't Protestants. I thought all Christians who aren't Roman Catholic or Eastern Orthodox are Protestants. Who's right?

—Bill

Q. What's the difference between fundamentalists and evangelicals?

—Elaine

A. The answers to these two questions overlap, in part because terms can have more than one meaning, as is the case with the word *Protestant.*

Catholic monk Martin Luther nailed his reform-seeking "Ninety-five Theses" to the church door in Wittenberg, Germany, during 1517. After he was unable to convince the Roman Catholic Church to adopt any of his points, he created a new church which became known as the Evangelical Church.

To this day, the church Luther started remains known in Germany as the Evangelical Church, while in the United States it goes by the name *Lutheran. Evangelical* comes from a Greek word meaning "to proclaim."

The four Gospel writers are known as the "evangelists" because they proclaimed the news about Jesus Christ.

As various other reformers tried to make changes in church practices over the years, they adopted the word evangelical for their own use. Some two hundred fifty years after Luther, followers of Methodism's founder John Wesley used the term to describe their philosophy. Evangelicals became seen as individuals emphasizing a personal experience of salvation instead of placing greater importance in sacraments such as Holy Communion, baptism, and the like. As they have developed, evangelicals came to believe they have a responsibility to spread the Gospel themselves and are often engaged in attempts to convert others.

Luther was successful with certain German princes who wanted to throw off control by both religious and higher political officials. To fight the spread of the reformed doctrine, the Holy Roman Empire, acting through the Diet of Speyer, issued an edict prohibiting these local princes and other leaders from determining whether their subjects would follow Catholicism or the new forms of Christianity in their towns and principalities.

Many of the reformers protested this edict and became known as *Protestants*. So originally, the term did not refer to someone who was not Catholic or Orthodox but to someone who disagreed with the empire's ban on the princes' choice of religion. The ban was imposed in 1529, about fifty years before Baptists emerged from the English Separatist movement. Baptists, therefore, are not Protestants in the limited sense of a group that opposed the prohibition; however, over the years the term has replaced evangelical as the label for that large group of Christians who are neither Roman Catholic nor Orthodox.

There are some three thousand different Protestant denominations so it's impossible to state what they all believe. Generally, though, they place more emphasis on hearing the word about Jesus preached or read, while Catholics and Orthodox Christians stress proper sacramental practice as the way of grace.

Over the years, as well, a movement developed to study the Bible with greater attention to science, history, and literary criticism. As a result, some scholars found what they believed were inconsistencies inside the Bible and with the knowledge of fields outside religion. This movement became popular in the late nineteenth century, much to the chagrin of traditionalists.

A group of these traditionalists met in Niagara, New York, during 1895 and established a list of principles to guide and protect their view of Christianity from this new form of Bible study. These principles became known as the five fundamentals.

These five fundamentals hold that: (1) the Bible is the inerrant word of God; (2) Jesus is divine; (3) Mary was a virgin when Jesus was born; (4) Christ's sacrifice on the Cross provided atonement for human sin; and (5) Jesus was bodily resurrected, ascended, and will return physically to the world.

Within Christianity, a fundamentalist originally was a person who adhering to these five principles. Since fundamentalists tended to be conservative in their religious and world views, the term *fundamentalism* began to take on the meaning of religiously conservative, which is ascribed to the word today.

In Christianity, a person can be a Protestant, evangelical, and fundamentalist at the same time, or none of them, or any other combination.

For some unknown reason, the proper day for keeping the Sabbath became an issue in Oklahoma City during 2007. Various sides exchanged letters on the editorial page, and I received this question from Chuck, who didn't identify his faith tradition, but the rest of his e-mail clearly indicated he believed Saturday was the only proper day.

Q. Where is the scriptural reference for Protestants to keep Sunday as the Sabbath?

—Chuck

A. The Bible does not direct Christians to observe the Sabbath on Sunday. This is why Seventh-day Adventists and a few other Christian denominations keep Saturday as the Sabbath, following the commandment's decree to rest on the seventh day and their understanding of the creation narrative in Genesis 1.

Early Christianity moved the observance to Sunday for two reasons. First, was the day Christ was resurrected. The resurrection is vital to Christian theology and signals God's gifts of forgiveness for sin, opportunity for eternal life, and loving-kindness.

Second, the earliest Christians considered themselves Jews experiencing the fulfillment of God's promises as set out in Hebrew scripture. But these Jewish Christians and the rest of Judaism had a falling out over many of the new Christian teachings, especially about the divinity of Christ. The Roman destruction of the Jewish Temple in 70 C.E. exacerbated that falling out.

In an attempt to define themselves as different from Jews, Christians dropped some older practices and modified others. One of the modifications moved the Sabbath observance from Saturday to Sunday.

Roman Catholic catechism teaches the original apostles moved the day of weekly worship from Saturday because Christ was seen as both the fulfillment of God's creation and the beginning of a new creation. Sunday, as the day after the last day of the week, symbolizes the end of the previous creation and, as the first day of the week, signifies the start of that new creation. After the Reformation, most Protestants kept Sunday as the Sabbath.

For believers following a literal interpretation of scripture, this is a difficult issue. Many Christian denominations, however, do not rely solely on the Bible for direction. For example, the Anglican Church developed its practices from the Bible, tradition, and reason. Methodists employ those three and their experience of the Holy Spirit. Tradition consists of the accumulated knowledge and experience of the church over the centuries and is the source of the Sunday observance of the Sabbath.

One of the difficulties I see in Protestantism is a tendency for Protestants to believe each denomination is interchangeable. They are inclined to attend the church of the day, the one with the music they like, or the dynamic preacher, or the most-fun youth group. Carol was concerned about a number of theological issues as she tried to determine where she would go to church. It was a refreshing emphasis on issues that matter in religion. Her printed question deals with one of those issues.

Q. I don't understand the differences in communion between churches. Some let everybody take it, and others don't. Some do it all the time and others hardly ever. Some treat the bread like God, and others say it's just bread.

—CAROL

A. The differences in the meaning of Holy Communion and practices surrounding the Lord's Supper are vast. It will take more than one column to deal with all the issues.

Grace is a bedrock principle of Christianity. Grace is God's act of pardoning a person who has sinned despite the fact the sinner does not deserves forgiveness. In Christian theology, no person can be saved except by God's grace.

By "saved," Christians mean God rescues them from sin; sin's consequence, which is divine wrath; and sin's end, which is eternal death. Christians also believe salvation provides them a new, intimate relationship with God. Understandings of how God gives grace determine how churches look at Holy Communion, also known as the Eucharist, meaning thanksgiving, or the Lord's Supper, after the meal Jesus shared with his disciples in the Upper Room before being betrayed.

On the issue of Holy Communion, Christian churches generally fall into one of three groups. One group, while believing grace is given in many ways, understands worshippers receive God's grace through the communion elements. Another group believes the elements do not contain the gift of grace; instead, adherents reenact Jesus' last meal before crucifixion as a way of remembering Christ's sacrifice for humankind.

The third group also rejects any teaching the elements bestow grace, but this group holds through the Lord's Supper humanity reaffirms the covenant God has made with them.

The first group calls Holy Communion a sacrament. A sacrament is a religious ritual with a tangible symbol signifying God's grace-giving. In the Lord's Supper, the bread and "fruit of the vine" (wine or grape juice) are the tangible symbols. Churches understanding the Eucharist as sacramental serve Holy Communion frequently because they believe God makes the gift of grace available often—even continuously.

For most churches in the sacramental group, it is possible for a believer to receive God's grace and then lose it. Frequent Holy Communion provides opportunities to regain grace. The Roman Catholic Church is indicative of this group.

The second group calls the Lord's Supper an ordinance but not a sacrament. In Christianity an ordinance is a command from God. When Jesus, the Son of God, ate the last meal before his crucifixion, he told his disciples to "do this in remembrance of me," Luke 22:19. Many churches in the command group serve Holy Communion infrequently—often just once a year. The annual service reminds members of Christ's act, as do celebrations of Easter and Christmas. Most Baptist denominations are part of this group.

For the command group, people receive grace when they understand they are sinners in need of rescue and so accept salvation from Jesus Christ. Often it is said that the repentant individual "accepts Jesus Christ as his personal Lord and Savior." Typically, this group believes "once saved, always saved."

The third group also recognizes Christ's command to remember him through the Lord's Supper and consider the act a memorial. Looking to Paul's epistles and the Book of Acts, this group finds early Christians practiced the memorial weekly; therefore, they serve the meal on every Sabbath.

For the memorial group, communion does not give grace, but it demands all participants examine their lives before partaking to determine whether they are acting as Christ instructed. This self-examination is expected to take place continually but certainly each week. Churches of Christ are representative of the memorial group. The memorial group tends to believe grace can be lost through a person's sinful actions.

Let's consider the communion question further.

Q. I don't understand the differences in communion between churches. Some let everyone take it, others don't. Some do it all the time, others hardly ever. Some treat the bread like God, others say it's just bread.

—CAROL

A. The differences in the meaning of Holy Communion and practices surrounding the Lord's Supper are vast.

Those variances begin with the nature of the communion elements themselves. The elements are bread and wine, but even here the various churches diverge. Some use only unleavened bread, while others may use that type of bread or a yeasted loaf. Many churches use red wine, but a number of Protestant churches use grape juice, and the Mormons use water. Some of the differences reveal how a particular church views these elements after they have been blessed.

Let's begin the discussion by looking first at a television show. "Extreme Makeover," a television program following a person undergoing plastic surgery, weight loss, wardrobe changes, and hairstyling, was popular a few years ago. The show's producers changed a participant's appearance completely: The hook nose became a petite, upturned sculpture; the paunch developed into rock-hard muscle; frumpy clothes converted to haute couture, and errant hair changed places with a magnificent mane.

But even after all those changes the made-over person remained essentially the same person. The participating woman was at the core who she was, and the altered man remained himself at the center of his being. Each one merely looked different.

Borrowing from Aristotle's ancient writings, in theological language we say the made-over person is still the same substance. The accidents of her looks have changed, but the core is still there. For Aristotle, everything in the universe was comprised of its substance—what it was at the core—and its accidents—how it appeared.

The substance of Jesus is the Son of God. When he walked the earth, Jesus probably had olive complexion and brown eyes. This complexion and eye color were part of Jesus' accidents. The substance of bread is grain. Bread's accidents are a brownish crust, a wheat taste, and a soft crumb.

In Eastern Orthodox and Roman Catholic understanding, when bread is consecrated, its accidents remain the same so it still looks, tastes, and feels like bread, but its substance miraculously changes from grain to the Son of God. In the Western Church, this is known as transubstantiation, meaning a change in a thing's essence. In the Eastern Church, it is known simply as a "mystery" and no explanation of the mechanics of change is attempted.

Because these churches believe the elements have become the actual substance of Jesus—his body and his blood—they insist the bread and wine must be treated respectfully and with tremendous reverence. In Orthodox and Catholic churches the consecrated elements will never be thrown away; they will always be consumed or buried in the earth.

As part of the Continental Reformation, Martin Luther rejected transubstantiation and substituted consubstantiation as the explanation for what happened to the Holy Communion elements. For Luther after consecration, bread was still bread in both its substance and its accidents, but the substance of the Son of God was also present. The reformer taught the presence of Christ was "with, in, and under" the bread. Luther admitted he did not know how this occurred. Consubstantiation teaches the substance of the bread and of the Son of God are present conjointly. The accidents of the bread are apparent, and the accidents of Christ are absent. Again, because the body and blood of Christ are believed present, churches following the Lutheran tradition treat the elements with respect.

Other Protestant groups, such as United Methodists, reject both transubstantiation and consubstantiation. Bread is bread throughout the service, but blessing the bread with the Words of Institution invites Christ to be present with the worshippers as the elements are shared.

In this case, because the bread and juice are believed never to have become the substance of Christ, leftover elements may be discarded without concern. Typically, leftover bread is fed to the birds and juice is drunk, saved, or poured down the drain.

Yet other groups, such as Southern Baptists, teach that reenactment of the Lord's Supper is purely symbolic and commemorative. For this group, when Jesus said, "This is my body" while holding the bread at the Last Supper, he was speaking only metaphorically. Jesus is not specially present in the elements or the congregation except as the Son of God is always near. Here again, leftover elements can be discarded since they were never considered the body or blood of Christ.

Let's discuss the last of Carol's questions about communion.

Q. I don't understand the differences in communion between churches. Some let everybody take it, and others don't. Some do it all the time and others hardly ever. Some treat the bread like God, and others say it's just bread.

—CAROL

A. The practice of allowing any worshipper to receive the bread and cup of the Lord's Supper is known as "open communion." The contrary custom of limiting the elements to certain individuals is known as "closed communion."

Open communion is practiced by many Protestant churches, including the United Methodist Church, Presbyterian Church USA, Christian Church (Disciples of Christ), and Reform Church in America. Typically, these denominations offer the elements to anyone who has faith in Christ.

Most often age is not a consideration, although some churches insist a child understand what she is doing before partaking. Some require baptism before participation in the Eucharist.

Closed communion is the rule in Eastern Orthodox, Roman Catholic, and many Baptist churches, as well as in the Church of Jesus Christ of Latter-day Saints. In the Orthodox and Roman Catholic traditions, right belief is required and that necessitates expressing faith in the manner these churches teach. In the Orthodox Church, infants are given the Eucharist immediately following their baptisms; therefore, communion is not limited by age.

In the Roman Catholic Church, a person receiving the Eucharist is to have engaged in the Sacrament of Reconciliation prior to the ritual. Reconciliation requires confession. Sins are not confessed until a child reaches the age of accountability, otherwise known as the age of discretion, at the end of his seventh year. Children younger than eight, therefore, do not receive the Lord's Supper.

While Baptist practice varies because of the autonomy of local congregations, many Baptist churches reserve communion not only for baptized believers but also for members of the local church. In Baptist churches, the Lord's Supper is not seen as a sacrament capable of bestowing grace. It is instead understood as the carrying out of Jesus' command to remember him through the re-enactment of the Last Supper. It is also viewed as the expression of membership in the community. Individuals who are not members of the local church are not members of the community.

Among Mormons taking the sacrament is understood as a renewal of the covenant a church member made with God at baptism. Since the LDS Church does not accept other church's baptisms, only Mormons may partake. Because the church practices believer's baptism, children under the age of eight do not receive the sacrament.

When I was Roman Catholic the Eucharist was still served "in one kind," meaning the congregation received the bread but not the wine. Since then, the Catholic Church has gone to serving "in both kinds," the bread and the wine, to the people. Protestant churches have served both since the Continental Reformation, but many choose to substitute grape juice for wine.

Q. I'm Catholic and attended a Methodist church with a friend and was impressed the minister invited everyone to receive Holy Communion. But I was surprised grape juice was served instead of wine. Isn't wine supposed to be used?

—Ray

A. For centuries, wine was the beverage used when Christians celebrated Holy Communion. The introduction of grape juice by some Protestant churches is a fairly recent development founded on America's one-time penchant for the temperance movement.

The biblical direction for remembering Christ's atoning sacrifice through reenactment of the Lord's Supper is found in four places. The oldest is Paul's recitation of the communion liturgy. After saying Jesus blessed bread and gave it to the disciples, Paul also reported Jesus "took the cup, saying, 'This cup is the new covenant in my blood; do this, whenever you drink it, in remembrance of me,'" First Corinthians 11:25. The accounts in the Synoptic Gospels, Matthew, Mark, and Luke, repeat the use of the word "cup" and use the phrase "fruit of the vine" to refer to the liquid Jesus used.

The lack of actual scriptural use of the word "wine" in the reports of Jesus' institution of Holy Communion led some Protestants in the latter half of the nineteenth century and the early twentieth century—when the temperance movement was at its zenith—to abandon the use of alcoholic wine because they believed it was hypocritical to work for abolition of liquor sales while serving an inebriating beverage in church, no matter how small the amount. The argument then—which continues today—was since the Bible does not use the Greek word *oinos,* referring to traditional wine, Jesus may have used "new wine" as the "fruit of the vine" in the cup. New wine would have been "pure grape juice," according to liquor opponents.

On the other side of the question, churches using traditional wine call attention to the fact the Lord's Supper occurred during Passover in March or April, which fell nine or ten months after the regular post-Pentecost grape harvest in the Holy Land. Natural grape juice pressed in June would have fermented by Passover. This group also points out Hebrew practice then, as today, was to serve fermented wine with the meal.

Frances Willard, leader of the Women's Christian Temperance Union, staunch member of the Methodist Episcopal Church, and sister of a brother suffering from alcoholism, pushed hard for the use of grape juice to help alcoholics avoid temptation. However, prohibitionists' early efforts to remove alcohol from communion were unsuccessful because as grape juice aged, it fermented and became wine naturally. With a limited grape harvest season, juice was produced in a four-month time frame. During the other eight months of the year, the juice became wine.

In 1869, a New Jersey dentist and former Wesleyan Methodist pastor named Thomas B. Welch applied Louis Pasteur's new germ-killing pasteurization process to grape juice. The juice did not ferment. Immediately Welch offered his "unfermented wine" for church use. The church declined on the grounds alcoholic wine was required.

Welch, also a commissioned police officer for the purpose of closing illegal taverns and destroying illicit liquor, persevered over many years and eventually replaced traditional wine in the Wesleyan church with his grape juice. Widespread use of Welch's "communion wine" would have to wait for the turn of the century. In the meantime he founded Welch Grape Juice Co.

After an initial reluctance to use unfermented grape juice as part of the Eucharistic celebration, today Protestant churches serving juice have decided their Christian duty to help alcoholics avoid sin trumps what they perceive as a "mere legalism" for the use of wine. With the perceived lack of explicit biblical direction to use wine as opposed to any other beverage made from the "fruit of the vine," those churches question the authority of that legalism.

On Mormonism

P.T. wrote a very polite e-mail (and a thank you after the column appeared). Little did he know he would set off a firestorm from coast to coast. My rule of thumb is no more than three columns in a row on the same religion or topic. I could still be writing about the Church of Jesus Christ of Latter-day Saints given the volume of mail for and against.

Q. What is the difference between a cult and a religion? Is Mormonism a cult, as is widely taught in some circles?

—P.T.

A. *Cult* comes from a Latin word which means to cultivate, as in cultivating crops. Romans began to understand one grammatical version of the word to mean "adoration" or "worship," either because appeasing the deities of rain and fertility was considered essential to farming or because religious adoration generally was seen as a way of cultivating favor with the gods.

Ancient religions were mostly polytheistic, but some worshippers chose to place special religious emphasis on a single god. For example, participants in the Greek-based Eleusinian Mysteries highlighted Demeter, the goddess of grain and agriculture. In the second century B.C.E., the drunken orgy known as bacchanalia erupted in Rome, where Bacchus, the hedonist god of wine, was revered by participants.

In each case, these participants continued to worship the pantheon of ancient gods, but their groups stressed the importance of a specific deity. These groups became known as cults. The word *cult* bore neither positive nor negative connotations.

Over time, the word came to be applied to any religious group headed by a charismatic leader with a new and unorthodox expression of faith.

Because of these unorthodox beliefs, the new factions often found themselves at odds with existing religious hierarchies.

From there, the word took on multiple personalities. In some instances, the term is very positive. In others, it is among the most negative criticisms to be leveled against a group of believers. In still other contexts, it has been a term social scientists have used to discuss small groups of religious adherents in a geographical area.

Looking for a positive use of the term, we find in the Roman Catholic Church various cults developed to give special attention to a saint or to further a particular worship practice. The "Cult of Mary" is one of these groups, which does not worship Mary but gives her special attention as the mother of Jesus.

In the 1970s, the People's Temple led by Jim Jones was identified as a *cult* in the negative sense of the word even before the group murdered a congressman and committed mass suicide. Cult as used in this context means a group which seeks total, exclusive, and malevolent control over the lives of its members under the guise of religious practice.

Languages not influenced by Latin have a term for cult, as well. As the term came to be used in its various guises and translations, it was applied to many religions widely accepted today. Christianity was originally seen as a cult arising from Judaism. Islam was viewed as a cult in opposition to the then-existing pagan religion of the Arabian peninsula. Buddhism was understood as a cult coming from what today is called Hinduism.

Oddly enough, there is no universally agreed upon definition of *religion*. Commonly, however, religion is seen as a set of beliefs involving the divine, with attendant rituals and practices. The teachings give the religion's adherents guidance for living.

A cult seems to be understood today as an eccentric part of a larger religion. The term has taken on such negative connotations it is best not used when attempting to bridge differences between groups.

When Joseph Smith founded the Church of the Jesus Christ of Latter-day Saints, commonly referred to as the Mormons, in 1830, the church was a cult in the sense of a group led by a charismatic leader with a new and unorthodox religious expression, much as Christianity was seen as a cult in the early years after Jesus' death. Today, the well-established church with some eleven million members worldwide—more than the United Methodists but fewer than the Southern Baptists—can no longer be labeled a cult.

When this answer was published to Nathan's question, he was most displeased. More of his questions and statements are included elsewhere—especially in the section "On Methodism."

Q. This is in regard to your column, addressing the question of whether or not Mormonism is a cult. My dictionary defines a cult as "a religion or religious sect generally regarded to be extremist or false."

Obviously, to properly address the question one must determine what is regarded as "false." As a Christian, my authority is the Word of God as contained in the Bible.

Scriptures clearly define Jesus as the Son of God and the Lord and Savior of those who believe in him. Mormons reject Jesus as such and cannot therefore be called "Christian."

—Nathan

A. Neither *Webster's New Universal Unabridged Dictionary* nor the *Harper Collins Dictionary of Religion* agrees with your definition of *cult* as a false religion, although the third explanation for the word in the *Random House Webster's College Dictionary* tracks your definition.

Typically, the judgment that beliefs of a so-called cult are false is made by opponents of the particular group. As my abbreviated history of the word's use tried to show, the term did not originate with this connotation of falsity. *Cult* continues to be used today in positive, negative, and neutral ways.

We also must be careful in using the term *Christian* as a synonym for the word *truth* and *non-Christian* as a synonym for *false.* There can be many truths in religions that are not Christian. Teachings of a faith are not automatically or completely false because the tradition is not Christian. And, as shown in the tremendous split of denominations within Christianity, not every one of Christendom's competing doctrines or conflicting teachings is necessarily true. Regardless, members of the Church of Jesus Christ of Latter-day Saints will tell you they are Christian.

Your premise that Mormons practice a false religion because they reject Jesus as Son of God and Lord and Savior is mistaken. As a person might suspect from the church's name, the Church of Jesus Christ of Latter-day Saints accepts Christ.

On New Year's Day, 2000, the First Presidency and Quorum of the Twelve Apostles, which constitute the leadership of the Mormon Church, issued a lengthy statement about Christ. In part they said, "We solemnly testify that His life, which is central to all human history, neither began in Bethlehem nor concluded on Calvary. He was the Firstborn of the Father, the Only Begotten Son in the flesh, the Redeemer of the world."

The scriptures of what adherents often call the LDS Church are the Bible, the Book of Mormon, *Pearl of Great Price,* and *Doctrine and Covenants.*

Christians believe that Hebrew scripture, known to them as the Old Testament, refers to Christ, especially in the books of the prophets. Obviously, the New Testament contained in the Christian Bible refers to Jesus explicitly and proclaims him as Son of God, Lord, and Savior.

The Book of Mormon likewise refers directly to Jesus. First Nephi is the first book within the Book of Mormon, and it refers often to the Messiah, including when the Prophet Nephi, in a vision, sees the Virgin Mary with her newly born child, and is told, "Behold the Lamb of God, yea, even the Son of the Eternal Father!" First Nephi 11:21.

The Book of Mormon also contains this statement attributed to Jesus: "Behold, I am he who was prepared from the foundation of the world to redeem my people. Behold I am Jesus Christ. I am the Father and the Son. In me shall all mankind have life, and that eternally, even they who shall believe on my name; and they shall become my sons and my daughters," Ether 3:14.

In the Book of Helaman within the Book of Mormon, Samuel the Lamanite explains that he prophesies so "ye might know of the coming of Jesus Christ, the Son of God, the Father of heaven and of earth, the Creator of all things from the beginning; and that ye might know of the signs of his coming, to the intent that ye might believe on his name. And if ye believe on his name ye will repent of all your sins, that thereby ye may have a remission of them through his merits," Helaman 14:12-13.

My copy of the Book of Mormon is 531 pages long. It contains about five hundred fifty references to Jesus in keeping with the excerpts quoted here. The other Latter-day Saint scriptures also refer to Jesus. For example, *Doctrine and Covenants* states, "And as many as repent and are baptized in my name, which is Jesus Christ, and endure to the end, the same shall be saved. Behold, Jesus Christ is the name which is given of the Father, and there is none other name given whereby man can be saved . . . ," D&C 18:22-23.

The *Pearl of Great Price* contains the Church's "Articles of Faith," the first of which professes belief "in God, the Eternal Father, and in His Son, Jesus Christ, and in the Holy Ghost." The third article states Mormons believe "that through the Atonement of Christ, all mankind may be saved, by obedience to the laws and ordinances of the Gospel."

A person may disagree with Latter-day Saint teachings but cannot correctly contend that Mormons reject Jesus as Son of God, Lord, and Savior.

Post script: While many people wrote to complain about my article on the LDS Church and Christ, many more readers, mostly Mormons, wrote thanks for "someone finally doing his research." The e-mails and letters included stories about Mormon children coming home from school crying because fellow students or teachers had told them they weren't Christian. I was most appreciative of an e-mail from John Jacobsen, president of the Mormons' Oklahoma Stake. Again, as with the Muslims, I found the people most affected were not the ones I was writing to. Instead, many of the Mormons wrote they saw hope for future relations with other followers of Christ.

Each column lists my e-mail and regular mail addresses for asking questions. Margaret is one of the few people who sent regular letters. She very kindly suggested I missed the point of an earlier question and rephrased what she believed the question was. Hers is the type of honest, well-mannered conversation we need more of as we try to understand one another.

Q. I wish you would point out the differences between historic, biblical Christianity and what the Church of Jesus Christ of Latter-day Saints really teaches. I am a conservative Christian who believes the Bible is the final authority and feel the Mormons have added to and changed the scriptures.

—Margaret

A. Almost every one of the hundreds of different Christian groups claims to follow historic, biblical Christian teachings. They do not agree on all those teachings.

Given this state of affairs, it can be difficult to find consensus on Christian teaching; however, it is possible to recognize differences between the Church of Jesus Christ of Latter-day Saints, sometimes known to adherents as the LDS Church, and other New Testament groups, just as we can see variation among Southern Baptists, Roman Catholics, United Pentecostals, and other Christian churches. Given the breadth of the subject matter, only a few topics can be addressed in a single newspaper column.

The obvious difference between the LDS Church and other New Testament churches is the Mormons' use of the Book of Mormon, subtitled "Another Testament of Jesus Christ." The Book of Mormon teaches Jesus came to the Western Hemisphere after his time in the Holy Land and preached his gospel to certain tribes here, although these teachings were lost with the destruction of those tribes until reclaimed by Joseph Smith. From the Book of Mormon, Latter-day Saints teach the New Jerusalem referred to in the biblical Book of Revelation will be established on the North American continent, while most other New Testament groups do not pinpoint a location or say the site will be the current Jerusalem.

Following Paul's epistles, Christians generally teach an individual's ultimate salvation is a matter of God's grace. Denominations differ on what is required of human beings as a result of this gift. Mormons rely on the biblical James 2:17, which states faith without works is dead.

For the LDS Church, God's grace opens the door to salvation, but once inside believers are required to engage in certain works, defined as keeping God's commandments and performing prescribed ordinances. Those ordinances include baptism by immersion. Throughout Christianity, churches disagree on the need for immersion, with less conservative groups tending toward sprinkling or pouring water on the congregant's head and more conservative following complete submersion in water. Mormons provide baptism only after believers reach the age of accountability and can choose for themselves to follow the church's teachings.

The LDS Church also practices baptism for the dead. In this practice, a current adherent is baptized in the name of a deceased person who was not able to receive the Gospel message as understood by the Mormons. The church finds support for such baptisms in First Corinthians 15:29, where Paul mentions baptism of the dead.

Mormons believe God has a plan for the world's salvation. For humans, this plan involves three stages. The first is "premortal life," in which human spirits live in Heaven before birth as human beings. These premortal souls may answer the Deity's call to follow the divine plan. Among the writings where the church finds support for this understanding is Isaiah 49:1, in which the prophet says, "Before I was born, the Lord called me." Other New Testament churches do not teach the concept of premortal existence.

The plan's second stage involves mortal life in which people find themselves today. Here, individuals may choose to follow Christ and prepare to be worthy of eternal life, according to Mormon teaching. The final stage is life after death. Following the biblical Book of Revelation, the LDS Church teaches a deceased person's soul stays in Heaven or Hell, waiting for Christ's Second Coming and universal resurrection.

At resurrection, individuals will be judged. Those receiving God's grace and performing the works necessary for salvation will find a place in the "celestial kingdom," where they will be with God the Father and Jesus Christ, according to Mormon teaching. Those judged honorable but "blinded by the craftiness of men," *Doctrine and Covenants* 76:75 will inherit the "terrestrial kingdom," where they will be in the presence of Jesus but will not know the fullness of God the Father.

This teaching is reminiscent of the two-fold blissful existence taught by Jehovah's Witnesses who believe an elect one hundred forty-four thousand believers will spend eternity in a heavenly existence with God, while other adherents judged acceptable will live in the New Jerusalem on earth. Mormons also teach those who have not received Christ's gospel will be redeemed from Hell and placed in the "telestial kingdom," where they will know neither the Father nor the Son but will be in the presence of the Holy Spirit.

While most other Christian groups do not teach a three-part Heaven, Mormons say they find support for the concept in First Corinthians 15:40-41, in which Paul speaks of heavenly bodies after resurrection. He describes such bodies as each having their own beauty, as the sun, the moon, and the stars have separate beauty.

Finally, under Mormon doctrine, those who chose an evil existence in mortal or premortal life will be known as the *sons of perdition*, "doomed to suffer the wrath of God, with the devil and his angels in eternity," D&C 76:33.

Elaine was working on her family tree and discovered a wealth of information through the Church of Jesus Christ of Latter-day Saints. She is not a member of that church.

Q. Why are Mormons so interested in genealogy?

—ELAINE

A. The Church of Jesus Christ of Latter-day Saints, whose members are known as Mormons, practice what are known as the Ordinances for the Dead. Besides bringing the living to salvation, the Latter-day Saints believe they are responsible for redeeming those who did not have an opportunity to hear the message and convert for their own "exaltation."

Exaltation is defined by *Doctrine and Covenants,* one of the four scriptural books of Mormonism, as a state of immortality in which believers and their families live eternally in God's presence. The most well-known of these ordinances is vicarious baptism for people who lived in the past. Mormons find direction for this posthumous baptism in Paul's first letter to the Corinthians, in which he defends the concept of resurrection, in part, by asking, "Else what shall they do which are baptized for the dead, if the dead rise not at all? Why are they then baptized for the dead?" First Corinthians 15:29.

Baptism of the dead is also based on scriptures in the Book of Mormon and others in the Christian Bible, including the books of Malachi, First Peter, and the Gospel of John, which says, "[T]he dead shall hear the voice of the Son of God: and they that hear shall live." John 5:25.

To make sure their dead ancestors have the opportunity for exaltation, Latter-day Saints construct genealogical charts to identify family members so the Ordinances for the Dead may be performed for them.

This question came from Nathan, whom I discussed earlier. I've removed the more belligerent language and presented his issue, but I'm sure he will still be upset I haven't given space to all his arguments.

Q. Mormons claim to have new scriptures and add to the Christian Bible with their own revelations. Read what the Christian Bible says about adding to Scripture in Deuteronomy 4:2. Indeed, in Revelation 22:18-19, Jesus himself states it is wrong to add to "the book," the entire Bible.

—Nathan

A. Most Christians probably agree that the biblical canon should not be tampered with, but such action is not unknown in Christian history. Even before Mormons introduced a separate set of scriptures, Christians were adding to and taking away from the Bible.

Various Christians found no difficulty with the practice despite the Deuteronomy verse that you cite. That verse tells the Israelites, "Do not add to what I command you and do not subtract from it, but keep the commands of the Lord your God that I give you." This directive is given as God is about to reveal the law through Moses.

There are two difficulties with understanding this verse as prohibiting any additions to scripture. First, if Deuteronomy was compiled by Moses, as many claim, then it was written before thirty-four of the thirty-nine books as arranged in the Masoretic text of the Hebrew Bible which also comprise the Protestant version of the Old Testament, forty-one of the forty-six books in the Roman Catholic version, and forty-six of the fifty-one books in the Eastern Orthodox version. Deuteronomy obviously also came centuries before the New Testament was added.

If nothing could be added or subtracted after Deuteronomy, then we will have to content ourselves with the Samaritan version of the Bible, which included only the first five books. If Deuteronomy was written during King Josiah's time, as others claim, then we could have perhaps fifteen books in the Bible.

Our second difficulty arises from the Council of Jerusalem as reported in Acts 15. In that council, James, Paul, Peter, and other leaders of the infant church drafted a letter to Gentiles seeking to become Christians and informed them they would not be required to follow the law given in Deuteronomy which proclaimed believers must be circumcised and had to refrain from certain foods, such as pork. If the Deuteronomy passage means these commands could not be subtracted from the requirements for the faithful, then almost two thousand years of Christian practice has been mistaken.

The Revelation text you cite says, "I warn everyone who hears the words of the prophecy of this book: If anyone adds anything to them, God will add to him the plagues described in this book. And if anyone takes words away from this book of prophecy, God will take away from him his share in the tree of life and in the holy city. . . ."

We are mistaken if we believe the Bible, including the New Testament, came together in one piece at one time. The books of the New Testament were written over the course of about half of the first century C.E. and perhaps a bit of the second. The Book of Revelation, which is called the Apocalypse by some Christians, may have been the last of the group, but it may not have been.

Regardless of the time when Revelation was drafted by most accounts, the New Testament canon was not set until the fourth century. Others contend the full Christian addition to scripture was established sometime in the late second century.

When the exiled and isolated John of Patmos wrote the book near the end of the first century, he probably was aware of many, if not all, of Paul's letters and perhaps John's Gospel, but it is doubtful he knew of each of the other Gospels, the Book Acts, or some of what are called the "catholic epistles"—especially Hebrews, Jude, and James. John does not list the New Testament canon among the revelations he received. When John says, don't add to this book, he means the Book of Revelation, not the entire Bible, because he did not know what the full Bible was or would be.

If Revelation 22:19, prohibiting taking away, is read to apply to the entire Bible, then Protestants run into difficulties with Martin Luther and other sixteenth century reformers' removal of the books of Tobias, Judith, and First and Second Maccabees, parts of Esther and Daniel, and Psalm 151 from the Bible, among others. Those writings were found in the Septuagint, the Jewish translation of scripture into Greek which was read by non-Hebrew-speaking Jews before, during, and after Christ's time on earth.

Additions and subtractions may be ill-advised, but the Bible as handed down today is the product of many changes over the years. In the next "Our Faiths" column, we'll discuss why the Church of Jesus Christ of Latter-day Saints believes it is appropriate to use the Book of Mormon as scripture in addition to the Bible.

We continue with the question about Mormon additions to scripture.

Q. Mormons claim to have new scriptures and add to the Christian Bible with their own revelations. Read what the Christian Bible says about adding to Scripture in Deuteronomy 4:2. Indeed, in Revelation 22:18-19, Jesus himself states it is wrong to add to "the book," the entire Bible.

—Nathan

A. Last time, we discussed changes in the Bible over the years and the impact of the cited scriptures. This time we'll look at why the Church of Jesus Christ of Latter-day Saints believes the Book of Mormon is valid scripture.

At various times in Israel's history, the Hebrew community was divided by both internal and external forces. Such divisions occurred when Joseph was sold into slavery, when Hebrews moved because of famine, when the Assyrians took the northern Israelite kingdom into exile, and when the Babylonians took the southern Judean kingdom into exile. Not all of these people or their descendents returned to the land of Israel.

For example, genetic testing has shown diverse peoples of Ethiopia, modern Israel, and Judaism around the world are related. At the same time, peoples who are not direct biological relatives of the Israelites claim kinship through the workings of God. This is especially true for Christians, who believe they have been grafted onto the root of Judaism, as explained by Paul in Romans 11:17.

During the Babylonian Exile, the Prophet Ezekiel wrote that God told him, "Son of man, take a stick of wood and write on it, 'Belonging to Judah and the Israelites associated with him.' Then take another stick of wood, and write on it, 'Ephraim's stick, belonging to Joseph and all the house of Israel associated with him.' Join them together into one stick so that they will become one in your hand," Ezekiel 37:16-17.

The Church of Jesus Christ of Latter-day Saints believes the scriptures accepted by most Christians are symbolized by the writing on Judah's stick and the Book of Mormon and other LDS scriptures are symbolized by the writing on Joseph's stick. Interpreting verses that follow in Ezekiel, Mormons believe God has told them to combine the scriptures into a new and whole understanding of the Lord's way. "This is what the Sovereign Lord says: 'I am going to take the stick of Joseph—which is in Ephraim's hand—and of the Israelite tribes associated with him, and join it to Judah's stick, making them a single stick of wood, and they will become one in my hand.'" [Ezekiel 37:19].

The LDS Church also finds support in the New Testament. When Jesus is quoted as saying, "I have other sheep that are not of this sheep pen. I must bring them also. They too will listen to my voice, and there shall be one flock and one shepherd," John 10:16, Mormons understand they and other peoples of the Western Hemisphere are the other sheep. Whether as descendents of lost tribes or those who have been grafted onto the root the church teaches. Jesus' voice is in the Book of Mormon.

Mormons consider their additional scriptures to be prophetic and inspired by God, in keeping with Amos 3:7, which says, "Surely the Sovereign Lord does nothing without revealing his plan to his servants the prophets."

While most Christians do not accept the Book of Mormon, *Doctrine and Covenants,* or *Pearl of Great Price* as scripture, the LDS Church finds biblical justification for its belief that God continues to speak to the world through his prophets and through writings accepted by the church.

On Roman Catholicism

In some early columns, I tried to answer more than one question, but I soon discovered the issues were usually too complicated given the limited space. This question was part of one of those multiple-issue columns. The Second Commandment, by the way, prohibits the making and worshipping of idols.

Q. Why do Catholics worship statues in their sanctuaries? Doesn't that break the Second Commandment?

—Larry

A. Roman Catholics do not worship statues; instead, this ancient religion, which first sought to spread the Christian gospel before many people knew how to read, uses statues, stained glass, and other symbols in the same way the Bible is used.

The Bible tells the story of God and God's relationship to humankind. Religious statues and stained glass do the same thing for illiterate individuals and people who are visually oriented rather than verbally inclined. For a person skilled in their interpretation, these pictorial symbols tell about the birth of Christ, the creation of the universe, and the struggle of early Christian martyrs, among other things.

Whether a statue or picture violates the Second Commandment depends on the person viewing it. Does that person worship the image itself or simply see it as an aid to worshipping God?

Muslim mosques and Jewish synagogues typically don't contain pictorial representations of God, people, or animals to avoid the temptation to treat any such thing as an idol. Many Protestant Christian churches follow suit, but other Protestants join their Roman Catholic and Eastern Orthodox comrades in using symbols as additional teaching tools.

Ray's belief about Catholic worship is a common but mistaken one among Protestants.

Q. You said "Roman Catholics do not worship statues" but use statues as teaching tools. My difference with your comments lies not in the specific words but the apparent omission and appearance of political correctness I see in them. Are the statues worshipped as gods? No, they are not; however, the person who is represented by the statue is worshipped as a god.

—Ray

A. If a Roman Catholic church contains statues, they are typically one of three kinds: depictions of Jesus Christ, representations of the Virgin Mary, or portrayals of various saints. Like other Christians, Roman Catholics worship Christ as one person in the Holy Trinity; Christ, therefore, is seen as God.

As a former Roman Catholic, I found a common misconception among various Christians that Roman Catholics also see Jesus' mother Mary and the saints as gods and worship accordingly. Roman Catholicism does not teach or hold this belief.

Mary is honored as the mother of Christ, but Paragraph 971 of the *Catechism of the Catholic Church* states Mary is not to be adored or worshipped as are God, the Father, the Holy Spirit, and Jesus Christ. Mary, instead, serves as an example to believers of holiness, obedience, and hope. As the Roman Catholic Church sees it, she is the epitome of a faithful witness.

The saints, too, serve as examples of the holy lives God calls on all believers to lead. Again, the *Catechism* teaches saints are not gods but are individuals who have prayed and continue to pray in the afterlife for humankind.

Confusion about the place of Mary and other saints arises because Roman Catholics may address prayers to them. Such prayers are not an indication Catholics believe Mary and the saints are gods.

In ancient days, common people did not presume to speak directly to individuals of much higher status. Instead, the commoners asked another person whose status was between theirs and the higher person to speak for them. Saints may serve a go-between function for believers wanting to talk with God. The Roman Catholic Church continues this practice, although it also recognizes the ability of believers to pray directly to God, Christ, and the Holy Spirit. Most Protestants don't accept the need or desire for any intermediary and thus typically disagree with the ancient approach.

The *Catholic Catechism* also teaches the prayers of Mary and other saints have "immense, unfathomable" value and when combined with the prayers of earthbound believers may help to bring people to salvation. Catholics, therefore, pray to Mary and saints for this assistance. Many Protestants see salvation as a more individual experience.

While discussing putting this book together, my publisher remarked he was surprised I had not received a question about the concept of the Pope's infallibility. I'm surprised not to have received more questions about the Catholic Church, generally. When I was growing up, Roman Catholics seemed to be a favorite target of people who believed they strengthened their own churches by attacking others. Today's fashion has moved to other faiths. Here's my publisher's question.

Q. Please explain the Roman Catholic Church's doctrine concerning the infallibility of the Pope.

—Jim

A. Church doctrine on infallibility is greatly misunderstood. Roman Catholicism does not teach the Pope is infallible; instead, it views the pontiff as an instrument of the church's infallibility.

Catholicism teaches only God is completely infallible. Christ, as one person of the divine Trinity, conferred limited infallibility on the church, as Christ's body on earth. According to Paragraph 889 of the *Catholic Catechism,* this flawlessness was given "to preserve the Church in the purity of the faith handed on by the apostles. . . ." In other words, the church is correct when it teaches doctrine and morality. It does not consider itself perfect on matters of custom, history, or foresight.

Custom includes such things as the garments worn by priests or the language used to celebrate the Mass. Doctrine includes teachings about the Trinitarian nature of God, the purpose of the sacraments, and the nature of sin.

Infallibility cannot be understood as perfection on all matters or omniscience—knowledge of all things. It is limited to accuracy on matters of faith and morals.

As explained initially by the First Vatican Council in 1869, the Pope is empowered to tell the faithful what Catholic doctrine is, but he is not permitted to change existing doctrine. Once a dogma is announced, it is set forever because it is the expression of God's infallible word. At the same time, however, the Pope may alter church habits, such as the practice of abstaining from meat on Fridays.

The Pope is limited, as clarified in the Second Vatican Council of the early 1960s, to expressing doctrine that is part of "the deposit of revelation." Put another way, God has already revealed religious doctrine, and the church merely uncovers or rediscovers it. Vatican II does "not admit any new public revelation as pertaining to the divine deposit of the faith."

Off-hand comments made by the pontiff—even on doctrinal matters—are not deemed infallible. According to the *Catechism's* Paragraph 891, only a definitive proclamation bears the church's imprimatur and attendant correctness. A definitive proclamation requires careful study of revelation as contained in scripture and tradition and a well-reasoned presentation.

Vatican II explained further that the College of Bishops, when acting with the Pope, also serves as a tool of the church's infallibility, with the same restrictions. In both cases, the accuracy of doctrine comes not from the Pope or the College of Bishops, but from the whole church inspired and led by God, according to Catholic teachings.

Once a definitive proclamation of doctrine or morality is issued by the church, adherents are expected to give "loyal submission of intellect and will" to the teaching.

On Orthodox Christianity

Orthodox Christianity considers itself the oldest form of Christian practice. A native Greek friend says many of his countrymen are proud of family genealogies extending back to converts at the Pentecost when the Holy Spirit descended in "what seemed to be tongues of fire" and blessed the new church, as mentioned in Acts 2:3. David asks a question that allows us to explore this ancient faith tradition.

Q. You've often remarked about the Orthodox Christian Church. Can you tell us how it differs from Catholicism and Protestantism?

—David

A. Orthodox Bishop Kallistos Ware of Great Britain has said to understand the Eastern Church a person should look at Orthodox worship and its environment because worship is supreme while doctrine is secondary to the faith tradition.

Walking into an Orthodox Christian Church, you will notice an immediate and very beautiful difference between it and churches more familiar to us in the West. At the front of the nave—the area where the congregation worships—you will find an *iconostasis* separating the sanctuary—the place where the altar resides—from the rest of the church.

An iconostasis is a screen or wall containing dozens and dozens of pictorial representations of Jesus, the Virgin Mary, various saints, angels, and martyrs. Known as icons, the pictures are arranged in a particular order and contain well-defined symbols that together tell the story of the Christian gospels, the Bible as a whole, the faith of the church, and the devotion of the particular congregation.

Today some Protestants and adherents of other monotheistic religions condemn the veneration of icons as idol worship, but the Second Council of Nicaea, conducted in 787 C.E. long before the Christian church split into its many factions, issued a decree which stated, "We salute the form of the venerable and life-giving Cross, and the holy relics of the saints, and we receive, salute, and kiss the holy and venerable icons, according to the ancient traditions of the holy Universal Church of God, and of our holy Fathers, who both received them and determined that they should be in all the most holy churches of God." Orthodox churches continue in this Nicene tradition.

Twelve centuries later, the Orthodox still kiss icons, light candles for them, and carry them in processions. Adherents deny they engage in idolatry because they understand icons as an "open book" reminding them of the individuals represented and the actions they took. In addition, veneration is an act less than worship. But perhaps most importantly, the Orthodox believe icons are necessary to say their faith is and has been physically embodied by real people doing the real work of the Lord. Only because Jesus was incarnated may he be portrayed, in Orthodox understanding; therefore, icons of Jesus Christ and the Virgin Mary—known as the *Theotokos*—are statements confirming God took physical form. Not to have an icon of Jesus and Mary in an Orthodox church would be paramount to saying Christ was not God manifest in the flesh; he did not have a physical body, and he did not really exist.

Today's Orthodox Church agrees with the Second Council of Nicaea's statement calling for more iconography depicting Christ, Mary, and other religious figures because "the more continually they are seen in iconic form, the more are beholders lifted up to the memory of the prototypes and to an aspiration after them."

What is known as the *service* in Protestant churches and the *Mass* in Roman Catholic practice, is called the *Holy Liturgy* or *Divine Liturgy* in Orthodoxy. Unlike other Christian groups, the Orthodox Church always sings the Liturgy in various forms of chant, depending on whether the congregation is Greek, Antiochian, Russian, or another church within the Orthodox community. The word *liturgy* comes from the Greek meaning "the work of the public," and the Eastern Church views weekly worship as a way of the people experiencing heaven on earth. In fact, worship in the local church is believed to be matched in time by worship in heaven, so that heaven and earth come closer together than at any other moment.

Every Holy Liturgy includes the Sacrament of the Eucharist. The Orthodox use leavened bread and wine for communion elements and understand these components become the actual body and blood of Christ. Unlike the Catholic Church or many Protestant faith traditions, the Orthodox Church does not name this process as "transubstantiation" or "consubstantiation"; instead, the Eastern Church is content to say the event is a mystery known only to God.

Communion is closed, meaning it is served just to the Orthodox in keeping with Justin Martyr's second century explanation, "No one is allowed to partake but the person who believes the things we teach are true, and who has been washed with the washing that is for the remission of sins and regeneration, and who lives as Christ has commanded." Orthodox children are included in Holy Communion because God's grace is given to them regardless of intellectual understanding. In fact, a child's first communion may occur at her baptism.

Baptism is by immersion, but in a practice that differs from that of many other churches insisting on total submersion, the Orthodox Church requires the baptizee to be immersed three times, once for "in the name of the Father, amen," again for "and the Son, amen," and finally for "and the Holy Spirit, amen." While the baptismal wording used by ministers in other churches may state, "I baptize you in the name of the Father, and of the Son, and of the Holy Spirit," the Orthodox priest says, "The servant of God (baptizee's name) is baptized in the name of" and so on to make clear the grace afforded by the sacrament comes from God, not from the officiant. All sacraments are served with similar phrasing.

Infants are baptized because the Eastern Church reads Jesus' admonition, "Let the little children come to me, and do not hinder them, for the kingdom of heaven belongs to such as these," Matthew 19:14 to require it. Immediately after baptism in water, the child receives Chrism. *Chrism,* a special ointment, is the vehicle for bestowing the gift from the Holy Spirit, following the example of Pentecost nearly two thousand years ago. The priest anoints the child's forehead, eyes, nostrils, mouth, ears, chest, hands, and feet, saying "the seal of the gift of the Holy Spirit." The anointing itself is known as Chrismation and serves as confirmation in the Orthodox Church. In various Orthodox congregations, after Chrismation, the elements of Holy Communion are prepared in the usual way, combining bread and wine into a mixture that may be served with a special spoon. This mixture is served to the child. Other congregations reserve communion for the next earliest possible celebration of the Holy Liturgy.

Over its long life, the Orthodox Church has often found itself subjected to persecution. When the Ottoman Empire ruled the eastern Mediterranean world, a leader occasionally would demand destruction of all icons and other symbols and practices of the church to combat what was perceived as idolatry. During the Crusades, Western Church soldiers attacked Orthodox cathedrals as often as Muslim mosques. In more recent times, Communism ruled many of Orthodoxy's homelands and insisted on atheism. The Orthodox Church has endured. Three of the four ancient patriarchates lie in predominantly Muslim areas. The fourth sits in Jewish and Muslim territory. The ancient patriarchates are Alexandria, Egypt; Antioch, Syria; Istanbul, Turkey (formerly Constantinople); and Jerusalem. Together with Rome, the ancient patriarchates were sites of the early leaders in Christianity. Following the Great Schism of 1054, when Roman Catholics and Orthodox went separate ways, the four ancient patriarchates served as beacons for the faith.

Each patriarchate is considered a separate church with various congregations around the world. In addition, Orthodoxy has nine "autocephalous churches," that govern themselves and likewise have congregations around the world. They are Russia, the largest of all the Orthodox churches with some one hundred fifty million members, and in order of size, Romania, Greece, Bulgaria, Serbia, Georgia (former Soviet republic), Poland, Cyprus, and Albania. They are joined by partially independent churches in Finland, the former Czechoslovakia, Japan, China, and Sinai, the smallest with nine hundred members. The real difference among the churches is the language used. All worship is conducted in the vernacular—the language of the people.

There is not a separate American Orthodox church, as congregations in the United States relate to one of the ancient patriarchates or autocephalous churches; however, a movement has started to create an independent American Orthodox Church.

The severance of ties between the Eastern and Western churches is a pivotal event in Christian history. In Protestant churches emphasis is given to the Reformation, but little is said about the Great Schism. Eloise, a Protestant, wanted to know more about her faith's history.

Q. What caused the Orthodox and Catholic churches to separate, and will they ever get together again?

—ELOISE

A. The Great Schism came about after many years of arguments and reconciliations between Latin and Greek branches of Christianity. The disputes revolved around liturgical practice, differences in language, governing authority, and simple personality conflicts.

Liturgically, an issue arose as to what type of bread to use while serving Holy Communion—leavened or unleavened? Rome decided to use unleavened bread because the Latin Church believed Christ must have used such bread when he directed his disciples to remember him through the Last Supper's reenactment. The Last Supper is understood as having been a Passover meal. In Jewish tradition, matzah is used during the Passover seder to recall Hebrews could not wait for bread to rise as they rushed out of Egypt. Matzah, a flat, cracker-like bread, is made without leavening. The Greek Church insisted on leavened bread because when New Testament accounts said Jesus "took bread, gave thanks and broke it," the Synoptic Gospel writers and Paul used the Greek word *artos,* for "bread." *Artos* is the word used to denote "loaf" or "leavened bread." *Azymos* refers to "unleavened bread." Today, Roman Catholics use unleavened bread for Holy Communion, and the Orthodox use leavened loaves.

Translation difficulties between Latin and Greek certainly contributed to some of the animosity, but the real language issue concerned three words everyone understood: "and the Son." The First Council of Nicaea drafted a creed which stated, in part, "We believe in the Holy Spirit, the Lord, the giver of life, who proceeds from the Father. . . ." Sometime during the ninth century C.E., an unknown Spaniard added three words to the Nicene Creed, causing it to read, "We believe in the Holy Spirit, the Lord, the giver of life, who proceeds from the Father *and the Son. . . .*"

Eventually, this amendment made its way to Rome, where the Pope accepted it as an indication of Christ's equality with the Father as one of the three persons of the Trinity. Constantinople and other Eastern churches objected because an ecumenical council had not approved the change. The East believed that because such a council had carefully drafted the creed after tremendous debate over every word, only a council could modify the creed. The debate over this "filioque" clause has not been settled. The Orthodox Church proclaims the Nicene Creed without it, and the Roman Catholic Church has made the words part of its normal recitation.

The filioque debate raised another point of contention leading to the Great Schism: papal authority. Could the Pope simply accept the amendment despite its not being considered by an ecumenical council? The Eastern Church viewed the Pope, also known as the Bishop of Rome, as one of five equal bishops, with the other four sitting in Constantinople, Alexandria, Antioch, and Jerusalem. Because the Pope resided in Rome, headquarters of the Roman Empire, he was given special honor, but that honor did not provide him with control over of the other patriarchate bishops, in the eastern view.

Rome, on the other hand, understood the Pope as Peter's successor. The Apostle Peter was the first bishop in Rome; Christ had changed Simon's name to Peter, meaning "rock," and had proclaimed, "on this rock I will build my church," Matthew 16:18. As the successor to the rock, the Pope held superior authority, Rome said. The Greek Church argued the "rock" Christ spoke about referred to faith, and each of the bishops had faith in abundance. They also pointed out that James, not Peter, had been the church's leader in the earliest days in Jerusalem.

The debate was complicated by Emperor Constantine's decision to create two capitals for the Roman Empire, one in Rome and another in the newly renamed city of Constantinople. As bishop in "New Rome," the patriarch in Constantinople should also be given special honor, the Greeks said.

Eventually, barbarians overran Rome and brought an end to the western Roman Empire. Without governmental leadership to see that services were provided, legal controversies decided, and citizens protected, the Pope stepped in to fill the vacuum and assumed many duties not previously exercised by a Christian bishop. In the East, the Roman Empire remained intact, eventually taking a new name, the Byzantine Empire. The emperor remained the legal authority in the eastern Mediterranean. Bishops in the East saw the Pope's new civil responsibilities as a usurpation of power and viewed with suspicion any papal act that might extend his power to the East. Likewise the West questioned actions by the eastern bishops because of the emperor's powerful influence in church affairs. The West accused the East of "Caesaropapism," allowing the governing civil authority to control church doctrine and practice.

Over time, the territories of Antioch, Jerusalem, and Alexandria came under Islamic control, and the Bishop of Constantinople was seen as the sole freely acting Christian authority operating in the eastern Mediterranean. The Eastern Church believed this bishop should, therefore, take the title of "ecumenical patriarch" to acknowledge his greater responsibility of protecting Christian teachings in the Greek-speaking world. The Pope and the Western Church saw the title as a statement of the patriarch's power over all of Christianity, including the Bishop of Rome.

Other issues erupted during this turbulent history, including disagreement over whether men married before ordination could be priests. To this day, the Orthodox Church allows married priests, so long as they wed before ordination. The Roman Catholic Church requires celibacy.

In the middle eleventh century, a Roman delegation went to Constantinople in an attempt to repair relations and to work out a compromise concerning certain actions of the Ecumenical Patriarch. The wrong people were sent, and the wrong people received them. The conference's participants developed an immediate and intense dislike for each other, resulting in the Roman delegation delivering a papal bull excommunicating the Ecumenical Patriarch to Hagia Sophia, the patriarch's cathedral. The Ecumenical Patriarch, in return, declared the Roman delegates *anathema,* meaning "accursed and separated from the fold." These acts in 1054 are normally seen as the actual split, although others historians argue attempts at reconciliation continued until 1204, when soldiers from the Fourth Crusade sacked Constantinople and defiled Hagia Sophia, causing an irreparable break.

Various attempts at rejoining the two have been made over the centuries, the latest series coming with Pope John Paul II's visit to Orthodox churches, Patriarch Teoctist's trip to the Vatican, the Catholics' return of relics to Constantinople, and the Ecumenical Patriarch's attendance at John Paul's funeral. Reconciliation is a slow-moving process.

On Adventism

Sometimes you wonder why you do things. When this column appeared originally, I called Saturday the sixth day of the week instead of the seventh. Cesar, a Seventh-day Adventist minister, quickly called the error to my attention, while also sparing my bruised ego by saying he agreed with everything else in the column.

Q. Do Seventh-day Adventists and Jehovah's Witnesses celebrate Christmas and Easter? I've heard they don't.

—Dana

A. While the Seventh-day Adventist and Jehovah's Witness traditions both give special emphasis to Adventism—the Second Coming of Christ—they are different denominations with separate histories and discrete practices.

Seventh-day Adventists arose from the Adventist or "Millerite" movement in America after the Great Disappointment of 1844. William Miller, a self-made, itinerant preacher, used the Book of Daniel to predict Jesus Christ would return October 22, 1844, and cleanse the Earth. When that event failed to occur, most Baptists, Methodists, Presbyterians, and others who had joined the interfaith cause became disillusioned and left the movement.

A sizable group remained, however, and some of those people eventually formed the Seventh-day Adventist Church. The new church taught that Miller had misunderstood Daniel's prophecy, and that Jesus had actually moved *within* heaven from the Holy Place to the Most Holy Place on the date Miller predicted, according to Seventh-day Adventist teaching.

Seventh-day Adventists continue to await Christ's Second Coming on Earth but join many other Christian denominations in saying the time and date of the event are unknown. The church often refers to the anticipated day as "the Christmas yet to come."

Seventh-day Adventists do not find instruction in the Bible to celebrate either Christmas or Easter as distinct holy days. Believers are free to celebrate Christmas and Easter if they choose, and many do, but the church does not feel obliged to recognize those days. Seventh-day Adventists celebrating Christmas are expected to avoid the materialism seen in many people's remembrance of the day.

Seventh-day Adventists find biblical direction only to keep the weekly Sabbath, so it is the only holy day in the church's calendar. Seventh-day Adventists observe the Sabbath on Saturday, the seventh day of the week, in keeping with the Fourth Commandment in Exodus 20:11, while most Christian denominations have changed to Sunday, the first day of the week, as recognition of Christ's resurrection on a Sunday.

Jehovah's Witnesses made themselves known in America a generation after the institution of the Seventh-day Adventist Church. During Reconstruction after the Civil War, Charles Taze Russell taught Christ's Second Coming began invisibly in 1874. Russell predicted a forty-year "harvest" of the righteous leading to the beginning of the end of the world as people had known it. When World War I commenced in Europe during 1914, Russellites—as they were called until 1931 when the group took the name Jehovah's Witnesses—found proof of Russell's teaching. Subsequent wars and a view the world is disintegrating in evil have solidified the group's beliefs.

Russell corrected what he saw as mistakes in previous Bible translations with development of his New World Translation. He also wrote *Scripture Studies* to help believers understand what they read in the Bible. Russell's Bible translation and *Scripture Studies* are Jehovah's Witnesses' revered texts today.

A major difference between Jehovah's Witnesses and most other New Testament denominations is the Witnesses' rejection of the teaching of the Holy Trinity. That teaching holds God the Creator, Jesus Christ, and the Holy Spirit are three persons in one God. Jehovah's Witnesses agree the three persons exist but insist only the first is God. Jehovah's Witnesses understand Jesus as the "first creation" of God and thus truly the Son of God, but not God. The Holy Spirit is a force sent to intervene on God's behalf, according to the tradition's beliefs.

Because they find no continuing direction in the Bible to observe religious holidays, Jehovah's Witnesses do not celebrate Christmas, Easter, or any other special religious holiday except the Memorial of Christ's Death. On this day, which comes during the Jewish Passover and Christian Easter season, Jehovah's Witnesses share bread and cup as instructed by the Gospel accounts of the Lord's Supper.

On Quakerism

The Society of Friends, or Quakers, have always been a small group, but their effect on the American way of life has been enormous. They were the first religious group in the country to oppose slavery. They established the first penitentiary—the name indicated a place where criminals went to repent. They have been at the forefront of every peace movement in U.S. history.

Q. Why are Quakers called Quakers? I have heard their worship services do not include any music or preaching. What do they do?

—Lowery

A. *Quaker* is the informal term used to refer to a member of the Society of Friends. The group was founded in England during the mid-1600s by George Fox, Margaret Fell, and others.

The seventeenth century was a time of tremendous social and religious upheaval in Britain. Puritan Oliver Cromwell led a revolution that beheaded the king and the Church of England's archbishop. The people shortly rebelled against the Puritans, reinstituting the monarchy and the Anglican Church. Fighting continued.

Groups not adhering to either the Calvinist strictures of the Puritans or the tenets of the Church of England were caught in the crossfire and suffered legal and social discrimination. The Society of Friends was a target.

Many Quakers were jailed, including Fox who served six years in prison for believing in God differently from either warring group's teachings. The story is told that once when brought before the judge, Fox told the magistrate he should "quake before God" for what the legal system was doing. The judge turned the phrase on Fox and called him a "quaker." The name stuck.

Quakers teach that liturgy, sacraments, and other rituals found in most churches do not provide salvation. Instead, all believers must develop their own relationships with God. Such a relationship is possible because of the Inner Light within each person. That Inner Light is Christ, Quakers say.

It makes no difference whether everyone calls the Inner Light *Christ;* the Light is still present and the key to a relationship with God, according to Quaker teaching.

Quakers came into the American colonies early but suffered some of the same persecution as in England. In 1660, Boston Puritans hanged a Quaker mother of sixteen children because she criticized a local clergyman for lax theology.

After fellow Quaker William Penn founded Pennsylvania in 1682, where religious toleration was the law, members of the Society of Friends came in larger numbers. Remembering their history, Quakers remain among the strongest proponents of separation of church and state.

Quaker worship services come in two forms: programmed and unprogrammed. In the unprogrammed model, worshippers gather in a meeting house where they sit together quietly until the Holy Spirit moves someone in the congregation to speak. That person gives voice to what the Holy Spirit wants proclaimed and then sits quietly again until someone else is moved by the Spirit.

In this way, Quakers forgo "dead ritual" and listen for God's "genuine voice." On occasion, no one feels compelled to speak, and the meeting passes in complete silence. Such silent meetings are not seen as failures because quiet meditation is vital to the Quaker experience.

Programmed worship is practiced by some forms of Quakerism. These services include preaching and the singing of hymns but place great emphasis on congregants participating in worship by sharing inspirations from the Holy Spirit.

In both programmed and unprogrammed services, sacraments familiar to many Christians, such as baptism and Holy Communion, are not practiced. Quakers do not call their local organizations churches. They use the word *meeting* instead.

As with other Christian and especially Protestant denominations, the Society of Friends has divided into various groups over the years. The four major groups include the Friends United Meeting, which is the largest and employs programmed worship. In size, it is closely followed by the unprogrammed Quaker group known as the Friends General Conference. The Evangelical Friends International is slightly smaller and conducts programmed worshipped services; while, the smallest group, the Conservative Friends, holds unprogrammed services.

On Foursquare Gospel

Judy participates with my wife, Mary, in a needlework group. This question came from Judy through Mary after one of their meetings.

Q. I recently drove by a church called the Foursquare Gospel Church. I thought it was an unusual name and wondered what it means. What do they believe there?

—Judy

A. The International Foursquare Gospel Church came about through the work of one of early twentieth century America's most successful evangelists, Aimee Semple McPherson. Sister McPherson, as she was called by followers, was reared as a Methodist but became an atheist as a teenager. When she was seventeen years old, McPherson attended a revival to see how "crazy" the worshippers acted. The revival preaching led to her conversion as a Christian believer.

Not long after that conversion, she married the revival preacher, Robert Semple, and became a missionary with him until Semple died two years later. A second marriage failed because McPherson believed she was called to God's work while her second husband wanted a conventional wife.

Traditionalists opposed her work because many believed a woman should not preach. Others were afraid of her "hypnotic" effect on her listeners.

She persevered and was among the first evangelists to use the new medium of radio as a means of reaching her audience and became the first woman in the United States to obtain a broadcasting license. Foreshadowing telemarketing, she also used the telephone to make converts in ways not seen before.

During a 1922 revival, McPherson preached about a vision she had received similar to the Prophet Ezekiel's vision in the Bible. She saw four symbols that "squarely faced" the four cardinal directions, and from then on, she referred to the "Foursquare Gospel." The name was probably also influenced by her exposure to Ireland's Elim Foursquare Gospel Association.

Her four symbols represented church regeneration, baptism in the Holy Spirit, divine healing, and the Second Coming of Christ. She interpreted Ezekiel's symbols as Jesus in various aspects: savior, baptizer, burden-bearer, and coming king.

The first of the Foursquare Gospel churches was Angelus Temple built in Los Angeles. McPherson intended it to be a place where people would learn evangelism skills to take back to their regular churches. Instead, the followers remained and a separate denomination was born.

McPherson's church was zealously involved in ministry to the poor during the Great Depression and opened its doors to individuals of all races and ethnic groups—something rare for its day.

The Foursquare Gospel Church believes strongly in the power of prayer to heal, immersion water baptism, baptism by the Spirit evidenced by speaking in tongues, the inerrancy of the Bible, and the Second Coming of Christ. It also teaches fanaticism is contrary to God's will, and believers should act in moderation. While ministry with the poor and other good works are emphasized in the Foursquare Gospel Church, the denomination believes salvation is a matter of repenting and accepting the unearned grace offered by God.

When McPherson died in 1944, she had founded about four hundred Foursquare Gospel churches in North America, with approximately twenty thousand members. Today, the denomination has more than twenty thousand churches around the world, with about two million members.

On First Born Churches

I like Bob's sense of humor and attitude about tolerance.

Q. I'm curious about the Church of the First Born and General Assembly. I want to have a better understanding of the guy whose reserved seats at our high school football games are right next to ours. All I know is they use the Book of Mormon. I want to be tolerant, but he keeps talking about Oklahoma State and we're die-hard University of Oklahoma fans.

—Bob

A. There are various groups using some form of *first born* as the name of their churches. The one you are asking about is probably the Church of the First Born that is one of six churches claiming descent from Joseph Smith, the founder of the Mormon movement.

When an Illinois lynch mob murdered Smith in 1844, three contenders for leadership of the religious movement he founded emerged. Brigham Young is the most well-known today, and he led what would become the largest of the six churches, the Church of Jesus Christ of Latter-day Saints, headquartered in Salt Lake City. James Strang, a Mormon leader in Wisconsin when the murder took place, said Smith had prophesied the killing and named Strange as the successor. Many of his followers would eventually become the Reorganized Church of Jesus Christ of Latter-day Saints, which recently changed its name to the Community of Christ.

About twenty years after Strang began his movement, some of Young's followers pulled away from the Salt Lake City church and declared Strang was indeed the true successor to Smith. This group, however, did not accept all the teachings of the Community of Christ. They followed fellow

Utahan Joseph Morris, who was killed by a sheriff's posse in 1863.

The Church of the First Born accuses Young of having Morris murdered. The Salt Lake City church denies it. Morris's successor, George Williams, founded the Church of the First Born in 1865. The name came from a vision Morris shared with his followers.

The major theological difference between the Church of the First Born and other groups using the Book of Mormon as scripture is its belief in reincarnation. This is also known as "Baby Resurrection" because believers are reincarnated as infants rather than raised from the dead as full-grown adults as anticipated for the final resurrection.

Williams said he was the reincarnation of Cainan, father of the biblical Enoch. He also taught that Smith was the reincarnation of the Prophet Mormon, who compiled the Book of Mormon. Smith's earlier-life writing of the book made translation of the unearthed Golden Tablets containing the scripture easier. Smith, as the Prophet Mormon, was also the reincarnation of the New Testament's Paul, apostle to the gentiles, which explains why some of Paul's statements are found in the Book of Mormon, Williams said.

In the church's view of reincarnation, life is a time of probation. God expects each person to use each of the "multiple mortal probations" to improve earth and the lives of other people. Anyone who fails to make these improvements will be reincarnated "in the rear" of humankind. Those who do the work of improvement will be allowed to pick up where they left off when they are reborn.

Unlike either Hinduism or Buddhism, the Church of the First Born does not see this cycle of reincarnation as the continuation of a difficult life. It is instead a gift from God, and all members look forward to the final Resurrection when God will create the New Jerusalem, as prophesied in the biblical Book of Revelation.

There can be a great confusion in names among churches, and First Born may be at the top of the list. After the preceding column was published, I heard by telephone, e-mail, and regular mail from many members of other churches of the First Born. While the following article mentions some of the other First Born churches, look at the "On Native American Religions" section for a similarly named church that used peyote.

Q. I don't know what church the inquiry referred to in your last column, but I am sure that it was not the Church of the First Born. If the inquiry was indeed about a Mormon derivative, then your answer may be correct. But if the question had anything to do with the referenced church then it appears to be a clean miss since that church has no use whatsoever for the Book of Mormon and no belief at all in reincarnation.

—Jerry

A. As mentioned in the previous column, over the years different churches have taken *first born* as part of their names. The writer of the last question referred to the Church of the First Born employing the Book of Mormon. As you point out, however, there are other churches using first born that are not descendants of the Mormon movement.

First born is a popular name because the term is used in the New Testament as a synonym for Jesus Christ, especially by Paul. The Book of Hebrews also uses the term to refer to believers, as when the author mentions "the general assembly and church of the first-born, which are written in heaven," Hebrews 12:23.

The largest of those other churches taking the first born name is referred to variously as the Church of the First Born, General Assembly of the Firstborn, First Assembly and Church of the First Born, and similar names. The church is about the same age as the United States. "Followers," as members of the church are known, take a literal approach to the Bible, with many insisting the King James Version is the only legitimate translation of scripture.

Dress is modest. Women do not cut their hair. Worship services tend toward the spontaneous.

The characteristic bringing the church to the attention of others most often is the followers' belief in healing prayer rather than medical care. When a member becomes ill, the family calls for church elders. The elders anoint the sick person with oil and pray for healing.

The church trusts faith to cure unless it is God's will the ill person "sleep" until the promised resurrection of all true believers. They base this practice on the Epistle of James, which says, "Is any sick among you? Let him call for the elders of the church; and let them pray over him, anointing him with oil in the name of the Lord: And the prayer of faith shall save the sick . . .," James 5:14-15.

Other churches using first born as part of their name include the Church of the First Born of the Fullness of Time and the Church of the First Born of the Lamb of God. The Church of the First Born of the Fullness of Time was founded in Utah in the 1950s and has an extensive mission in Mexico. This church teaches that until the world follows the Ten Commandments exactly as reported in the Book of Exodus, Jesus will not return in the Second Coming.

The Church of the First Born of the Lamb of God is led by the Great Grand Patriarch. The Patriarch requires strict obedience to church doctrine. Anyone who strays from that doctrine is required to perform acts of repentance or face punishments which have resulted in criminal prosecutions in Texas and California courts.

On Churches of God

Oklahoma is home to a surprising number of church headquarters. This question concerns a relatively new main office in Edmond, a suburb of Oklahoma City.

Q. Recently my husband and I came across a new development in Oklahoma with a building identified as the world headquarters of the Philadelphia Church of God and the Herbert W. Armstrong College. We remember Armstrong's "World Tomorrow" programs, but we thought he was from California. What can you tell us?

—Belle

A. As you correctly recalled, Herbert W. Armstrong, the self-taught preacher who founded the Worldwide Church of God during the Great Depression, was headquartered in California until his death in 1986. Armstrong, and eventually his son Garner Ted Armstrong, used radio and television to teach an unorthodox form of Christianity opposed by many other New Testament denominations but which found a vast audience of converts over the airwaves. Originally, in fact, Herbert Armstrong's church was called the Radio Church of God.

The Armstrongs split over beliefs and practices in the 1970s, so when the elder Armstrong died, his son was not in a position to inherit the leadership of the Worldwide Church of God as planned originally. Instead, Joseph Tkach, a minister for three decades, took over as pastor general of the church. Shortly after he took the reins of the church, Tkach began to disavow many of the elder Armstrong's teachings and moved the denomination closer to traditional, evangelistic doctrine. This splintered the church.

Gerald Flurry, a minister in the Worldwide Church of God, founded the new Philadelphia Church of God in Edmond, Oklahoma, in 1989 to continue Herbert Armstrong's teachings. *Philadelphia* comes from a Greek word meaning "one who loves his brother." The Philadelphia Church of God has membership in the United States, Canada, Australia, New Zealand, and South Africa.

Following Herbert Armstrong's teachings, the Philadelphia Church of God rejects the Trinity which is integral to most other New Testament denominations. Instead, the church teaches the Godhead is composed of two persons: God, the father of Jesus Christ, and Jesus, the Son of God. The church teaches the Holy Spirit is not a separate person of God but the "power of God."

The Spirit is given to each baptized person so the new believer can do the works God demands through the Ten Commandments of Hebrew scripture and the "greatest commandments" of the New Testament, which are to love God and neighbor.

The Edmond-based church also teaches the lost tribes of Israel became the Anglo-Saxons whose descendants founded Great Britain and the English colonies of the United States. The British and Americans, therefore, have been specially endowed by God. Biblical warnings against falling away are thought to be directed at these two nations. This teaching is not unique to the Philadelphia Church of God and is known as "British Israelism."

The Philadelphia Church of God recognizes the Sabbath from sundown Friday to sundown Saturday and keeps seven annual holy days: Passover and the Days of Unleavened Bread, Pentecost, Feast of Tabernacles, Feast of Trumpets, Day of Atonement, and the Last Great Day.

Jerry is a retired minister who is a regular reader of "Our Faiths." The church he mentions, Crossings, is one of the fastest-growing in Oklahoma.

Q. I found your article about the Philadelphia Church of God to be most interesting. It causes me to ask, what is the difference in the Philadelphia Church and the Crossings Church, which is also Church of God, here in Oklahoma City? My recollection is there is a relationship with Anderson, Indiana, but not sure how.

—JERRY

A. Some two hundred groups use the name *Church of God.* While doctrine varies widely from group to group, these sects share a belief that Christianity has become too fragmented and needs to be reunited in one church. These groups do not call themselves denominations but each considers itself the vanguard re-establishing the single assembly of believers existing in the days immediately after the birth of the Christian church at Pentecost almost two thousand years ago. All adopted the name *Church of God* from Paul's reference to the company of early believers in his various letters.

Many of these groups started in the 1800s, when members of existing denominations—mostly Baptist and Methodist, but including some others—worried that their churches had become more concerned with denominational matters than with the basic message of Christianity. High on their list was a conviction that existing denominations had abandoned holiness, a belief that a member's life ought to be filled with practices pleasing to God. These actions are engendered when a believer receives the Holy Spirit.

With so many different groups using *Church of God* as their names, the churches are often distinguished by the addition of the town where they are headquartered or were formed. The Church of God (Anderson) is a voluntary confederation of believers headquartered in Indiana and was formed in 1880. While it does not have a historical connection to other churches of God, it shares many of the other groups' beliefs, which include the experience of holiness, seeing the Bible as the inspired word of God, forgiveness of sin through Christ's crucifixion and the repentance of the individual believer, and understanding God as present in the Trinity: Father, Son and Holy Spirit.

The Philadelphia Church of God, on the other hand, does not accept the Trinity, but sees God as two persons, the Creator and Christ. The Philadelphia Church of God follows the doctrinal teachings of Herbert W. Armstrong, one of the earliest broadcast evangelists, who formed the Philadelphia church's predecessor in the 1920s. The Church of God (Anderson) rejects many of Armstrong's teachings, such as recognizing Saturday as the Sabbath. The ministers of Crossings Community Church have connection with the Church of God (Anderson).

There are many other groups within the Church of God movement, such as the Cleveland, Tennessee; Huntsville, Alabama; Seventh Day; Holiness; and Original churches of God. These others usually share a history that began in North Carolina and Tennessee in the late nineteenth and early twentieth centuries. They place a greater emphasis on holiness and are generally known as part of the Pentecostal Movement, which will be discussed next.

On Pentecostalism

From my own experience as a teenager, I know Pentecostal services can be off-putting to individuals used to "traditional" worship. In a Pentecostal service, you may see individuals shaking as they feel possessed by the Holy Spirit, and there will be a lot of hand-raising and waving. People often begin to speak in tongues—giving voice to utterances others do not understand. There is tremendous power and energy in such services.

Q. We attended our future son-in-law's Assembly of God church and were stunned to hear people speaking in tongues during the worship service. We didn't know they did this, thinking it was a Pentecostal practice.

—Sue

A. The Pentecostal Movement is not limited to churches calling themselves by that name. The movement includes the General Council of the Assemblies of God, Church of God (Cleveland), Church of God (Original), Church of God in Faith, and the Elim Fellowship, as well as churches using "Pentecostal" as part of their names.

These groups see speaking in tongues or *glossolalia* as evidence a believer has been baptized by the Holy Spirit. A water-baptized individual who does not speak in tongues has yet to receive the Spirit and waits for "the fire" to come upon him.

This belief is taken from the second chapter of the Book of Acts, which reports the Holy Spirit descended upon the water-baptized church in Jerusalem by means of "what seemed to be tongues of fire" and enabled the disciples to "speak in other tongues." The doctrine is strengthened by the Book of Acts' tenth chapter account of the Apostle Peter baptizing

Gentiles with water after the Holy Spirit endowed them with the gift of "speaking in tongues," as well as by other New Testament passages.

The Pentecostal Movement began in the American South during the late nineteenth and early twentieth centuries as a reaction, in part, to a growing scholarly and scientific approach to interpreting the Bible. The Pentecostal Movement also opposed what its members saw as a trend away from "holy living" toward more worldliness.

Pentecostals understand the Bible as the inerrant and infallible word of God and refuse any effort to interpret the scripture other than literally.

Most Pentecostal churches call on their members to dress modestly. Many ask women to refrain from cutting their hair and to eschew make-up or other adornment. In light of this, some forbid the wearing of jewelry, including wedding rings.

The use of tobacco and alcohol is often forbidden because these substances are viewed as an affront to God's gift of life. Some Pentecostal organizations prohibit attendance at movies or ownership of television sets because of what is viewed as licentious behavior on the screen.

Pentecostalism is the fastest-growing religious belief in the world today, outpacing even the quickly increasing population of Muslims. Its growth is especially explosive in the Third World areas of Latin America, Africa, and Asia. In fact, many Pentecostal groups which formed in the United States now have the bulk of their membership in Central and South America.

On Churches of Christ

A number of movements over the years have attempted to recreate the "ancient church." Each group has tried to strip worship services and theology of anything not practiced or taught in the days immediately after the Pentecost following Jesus' ascension. Christianity celebrates that Pentecost as the day when the Christian church was born. The Church of Christ movement is part of that "ancient church" effort. Elaine's question was sent by that rare and beautiful thing: a handwritten letter.

Our grandson is marrying a lovely young lady of a different faith. She did not want a wedding in her church because instrumental music was not allowed. She also did not want to get married in our church. She wanted a backyard wedding. Would you please enlighten us on the beliefs of the Church of Christ?

—Elaine

A. Each Church of Christ traces its heritage through the Restoration Movement that swept the new American nation in the late 1700s and early 1800s.

Baptists in New England, Methodists along the Middle Atlantic Coast, and Presbyterians in the Appalachian Mountains, among others, grew distressed by what they saw as too much highlighting of denominational beliefs and not enough emphasis on what Christ taught and the earliest Christian church practiced.

Led predominantly by transplanted Scotsman Alexander Campbell and Presbyterian clergyman Barton Stone, some worshippers withdrew from their denominations and established individual, self-governing churches seeking to return Christianity to ancient practices and biblical teachings. They threw out all creeds, such as the Westminster Confession of Faith and the Apostles' Creed, and announced they had only one creed, the Bible.

They saw no reason to name themselves in any way other than as believers in Jesus Christ. Individual congregations, therefore, were called churches of Christ, disciples of Christ or Christian churches. In the beginning, these groups found it important to use lower-case rather than capital letters when referring to themselves, to avoid the appearance of denominationalism.

They opposed any organization not at the local church level alone. For example, the Restoration Movement believed the New Testament showed ancient churches engaged in mission work individually and did not form umbrella organizations for that purpose. The movement, therefore, eschewed mission societies in which various churches pooled their efforts for evangelism, charity, or any other work.

In 1906 and 1968, divisions occurred in the Restoration Movement, leading to three groups: Christian Church (Disciples of Christ), the most liberal, which has become a denomination in the traditional sense; Christian Church/Churches of Christ, the centrist group, which retains complete local church autonomy; and the Churches of Christ, the most conservative of the group and which you asked about.

Using the Bible—and giving great weight to the New Testament—each Church of Christ decides for itself what it believes and teaches. Despite this autonomy, there is a surprising degree of similarity among churches in practice and doctrine.

As your future daughter-in-law mentioned, Churches of Christ typically prohibit the use of musical instruments in worship. Members tend to read the Bible literally and to allow in church only those things the New Testament specifically authorizes. They find direction for singing in Ephesians 5:19, "Speak to one another with psalms, hymns and spiritual songs. Sing and make music in your heart to the Lord. . . ."

While the Old Testament mentions the use of musical instruments, the New Testament does not, so Churches of Christ practice only a cappella singing during services. Adherents often point out instrumental music was not used in Christian churches until the 600s, and the term "a cappella," meaning to sing without instrumental accompaniment, is Italian for "as in the chapel."

Churches of Christ tend to teach each person has free will to accept or reject saving grace offered by God. In keeping with this teaching, they believe predestination is limited to God ordaining that those who are righteous will be saved while those who are not righteous will be damned.

A person accepts God's offer of grace by being baptized, according to most Churches of Christ; therefore, only a person who has reached the age of accountability and can make such a decision may be baptized. Baptism is by immersion because it is believed John the Baptist submerged Jesus when baptizing him and because the New Testament Greek root of *baptize* means to "dip, plunge, or immerse."

While some Christian denominations believe "once saved, always saved," Churches of Christ typically teach a person may lose or reject the salvation he once accepted.

Churches of Christ do not consider themselves as Protestant, nor do they count themselves as Orthodox or Roman Catholic. They do, however, celebrate Holy Communion every week, using grape juice instead of wine.

Churches of Christ interpret literally First Timothy 2:11, which says, "I do not permit a woman to teach or to have authority over a man; she must be silent." Therefore, the congregations are led by male elders.

On Methodism

The issue of women in the clergy has been a hot-button topic since the church's birth. The ancient, non-canonical "Gospel of Mary Magdalene" displays some of the early disagreement about the place of women in the church. The Methodist Church passed a rule for the ordination of women in 1956. Half a century later, it's still controversial for some people.

Q. Methodists don't follow Scripture. Witness the admonition by the Apostle Paul writing to Timothy clearly elucidating God's plan regarding women, forbidding them to take authority over men. Methodist women pastors are in au thority over men.

—Nathan

A. The scripture you refer to says, "I do not permit a woman to teach or to have authority over a man; she must be silent," First Timothy 2:12. The Free Methodist, United Methodist, African Methodist Episcopal, and Christian Methodist Episcopal churches ordain women and enlist them as Sunday school and Bible study teachers. How do they justify such action given the passage you cite?

One of the remarkable things about First Timothy is that Paul says what he does or wants more often than what God wants, unlike other epistles bearing his name. The Methodist churches point out the letter does not say God prohibits women from teaching or having authority, just that Paul himself does.

In fact, women have been an integral part of God's work throughout the centuries. For example, Deborah served as judge over all of Israel. Mary Magdalene was an ever-present part of Jesus' earthly ministry. Rahab saved Caleb and his Israelite scouts, enabling the Hebrews to conquer Jericho. Lydia led Europe in converting to Christianity, and Priscilla traveled the Mediterranean as a hard-working missionary.

Occasionally Paul chose to conform to society temporarily to make converts. Witness his self-admitted "concession" in First Corinthians 7:6. Methodist churches see Paul's statement here as a concession to the patriarchal system of the day, just as his acceptance of slavery and advice to slaves to "consider their masters worthy of full respect" in First Timothy 6:1 was a concession to the forced-labor system of his day.

This comment was used for years as a justification for slavery in America, but Methodist churches and other Christians have condemned slavery as wrong. While Paul presents many important and useful teachings about God and human relationships with God, these churches believe Christianity cannot use Paul's concessions to the social practices of his day as guidance for our world and our worship today.

Paul's timeless teachings should control, Methodists believe. Among those teachings is Paul's statement of God's view, "There is neither Jew nor Greek, slave nor free, male nor female, for you are all one in Christ Jesus," Galatians 3:28. This was a radical concept in Paul's day, and one speaking of God's great love for each and every one of his created human beings. If there is no male or female, there can be no discrimination in ordination, these churches argue.

Methodism is not alone in ordaining women. The Evangelical Lutheran Church in America ordains women, although the Lutheran Church-Missouri Synod does not. The Salvation Army and United Church of Christ also have women ministers, along with other Protestant denominations. Eastern Orthodox, Roman Catholic, and Southern Baptist churches do not.

Of late, the Reform, Conservative, and Reconstructionist branches within Judaism have granted *semicha*, meaning "authorization," to women, making them rabbis, while Orthodox Judaism has not.

Within Buddhism, the Theravada school stopped establishing nuns many years ago, but the Mahayana tradition continues the practice.

The issue of homosexuality rises at almost every policymaking meeting of mainline Christian churches these days. While there is no consensus among the traditions on that question, most agree with the need to minister to all people.

Q. Methodists have been publicly reported to include unrepentant sinners practicing homosexual lifestyles in their fellowship. Scripture clearly condemns such behavior.

—Nathan

A. No one can speak for the United Methodist Church except the General Conference, which meets once each four years; however, I imagine the church would gladly confess to having unrepentant sinners among its congregations.

Specifically on the question of homosexuality, the United Methodist *Book of Discipline* states, "Homosexual persons no less than heterosexual persons are individuals of sacred worth. All persons need the ministry and guidance of the church in their struggles for human fulfillment, as well as the spiritual and emotional care of a fellowship that enables reconciling relationships with God, with others, and with self. The United Methodist Church does not condone the practice of homosexuality and considers this practice incompatible with Christian teaching. We affirm that God's grace is available to all, and we will seek to live together in Christian community. We implore families and churches not to reject or condemn lesbian and gay members and friends. We commit ourselves to be in ministry for and with all persons," *Book of Discipline,* Paragraph 161(G).

The church, however, does not ordain "self-avowed, practicing homosexuals," according to its discipline.

In keeping with the Ten Commandments, the Sermon on the Mount, and other biblical teachings, Methodists recognize lust, lying, jealousy, and nursing anger as sins, as well. It's fairly certain a few Methodists in last week's services and more in the approaching services have committed these sins and others, but the church does not believe this is reason for keeping individuals out of worship services.

The Gospel of Matthew reports when Pharisees asked Jesus' disciples, "Why does your teacher eat with tax collectors and 'sinners'?" he replied, "It is not the healthy who need a doctor, but the sick. But go and learn what this means: 'I desire mercy, not sacrifice.' For I have not come to call the righteous, but sinners," Matthew 9:11-13. The United Methodist Church, as many other churches, attempts to minister to the sinners called by Christ.

In her wonderful poem, "When I Say, 'I Am a Christian,'" Carol Wimmer said it well:

When I say, 'I am a Christian'
I don't speak with human pride
I'm confessing that I stumble—
Needing God to be my guide. . . .

When I say, 'I am a Christian'
I'm not bragging of success
I'm admitting that I've failed
And cannot ever pay the debt. . . .

When I say, 'I am a Christian'
I do not wish to judge
I have no authority. . .
I only know I'm loved.

Post Script: *"When I Say, 'I Am a Christian'" has been incorrectly attributed to Maya Angelou. Ms. Wimmer wrote it originally for Hi-Call Gospel Magazine. The poem has more verses than published here.*

The Amish have become an American symbol of religious devotion. While most of us don't want to share the lifestyle, we admire the strength of faith and the quiet resolve of these peaceful people.

Q. Where in the Bible do the Amish find the prohibition against modern inventions?

—Jimmy

A. The Amish are divided into various groups, but when we think of the band that with strictest view on the use of modern inventions, we are talking about the Old Order Amish.

The Amish were part of the Anabaptist Reformation of the sixteenth century. Anabaptist means "rebaptizer," and the group believed everyone baptized as an infant in the Roman Catholic Church needed to go through the ritual again as adults. Anabaptists taught infants did not know the difference between good and evil. Babies therefore could not sin and were not in need of the forgiveness accompanying baptism. Adults needed to be baptized to deal with their sins after the age of accountability.

Originally, the Amish were part of the Mennonites inspired by Menno Simons in Western Europe, but they split from that church over the issues of foot-washing and excommunication. A group led by Jacob Amman believed Jesus commanded foot-washing just as he had directed his followers to practice Holy Communion. They also believed errant church members should be excommunicated and shunned. Amman's faction became the Amish.

The Old Order Amish read the Bible literally. When the Apostle Paul urged the Christian church in Rome to "not conform any longer to the pattern of this world, but be transformed by the renewing of your mind," Romans 12:2 the Amish understood his direction to mean believers should remain separate from the unbelieving world. Separation is seen as necessary to protect proper worship of God and daily adherence to God's law. Members of the community who continue to violate church rules are shunned by others, a practice of separation known as *Meidung,* German for "avoidance."

They find additional support for their views about separation in Paul's second letter to the church in Corinth: "Do not be yoked together with unbelievers. For what do righteousness and wickedness have in common? . . . Therefore come out from them and be separate, says the Lord," Second Corinthians 6:14, 17. It is not that the Amish oppose modern conveniences; instead, they wish to remain separate from other people in the world because they fear contamination or corruption coming into their midst.

The Amish see using electricity coming through power lines running from the outside world's generating plant as a connection to the world scriptures tell them to avoid. Some Old Order Amish occasionally use electricity provided by batteries because the batteries are not directly linked to the outside world.

Since the Amish do not have a hierarchical structure, each church community develops its own rules—known as *Ordnung,* meaning "order"—concerning connection to the world around them, the use of modern inventions, proper social interaction, worship, and other religious matters.

Certain Amish fear that the convenience of modern inventions will tempt the community to put too much emphasis on material success, when their efforts should be directed toward worship and pleasing God.

On Unitarian Universalism

Recent surveys indicate Unitarian Universalism is the only so-called liberal religious denomination experiencing growth in the twenty-first century. The others—along with many mainline Christian denominations—are losing members at a rapid rate. This question allows us to consider this unique faith tradition.

Q. Unitarians don't seem to be religious. They're humanists. Why are they considered a church?

—ADELE

A. The Unitarians you write about have a long history among the world's religions and are part of a church known today as the Unitarian Universalist Association. Historically the Unitarian part of the name comes from the belief God is a single entity. This is the teaching of Islam and Judaism and was a principle taught by some church leaders in the earliest years of Christianity. However in the Christian church, Unitarianism fell to Trinitarianism at the First Council of Nicaea, which was convened at the urging of Roman Emperor Constantine in 325 C.E. Trinitarians drafted the Nicene Creed, which states there is one God in three persons: Father or Creator, Son Jesus Christ, and Holy Spirit.

The Universalist part of the name comes from rejecting the concept that only a few, select individuals will be saved. Universalism contends divine love will cause all people to be reconciled with God eventually. This thought was expressed by Origen of Alexandria, who lived during parts of the second and third centuries C.E. Origen wrote extensively on universal salvation and is considered among the first of the philosophical church fathers. Universalism has been rejected by the church at large at various times in Christian history—perhaps most spectacularly by John Calvin whose reform church taught God elected very few people for ultimate salvation. In the past one hundred years, however, Universalism has gained ground in mainline denominations.

Often under tremendous persecution, Unitarianism and Universalism developed as separate ideologies and churches until 1961 when the American Unitarian Association and the Universalist Church in America merged to form the Unitarian Universalist Association. It is often considered—and considers itself—among the most liberal religious organizations in the United States.

The church has no creed and does not require certain beliefs or practices. In 1986 the association added a statement to its covenant listing six sources where Unitarian Universalists draw their individual faiths. They look to "Jewish and Christian teachings which call us to respond to God's love by loving our neighbors as ourselves; [h]umanist teachings which counsel us to heed the guidance of reason and the results of science, and warn us against idolatries of the mind and spirit; [and] [s]piritual teachings of earth-centered traditions which celebrate the sacred circle of life and instruct us to live in harmony with the rhythms of nature. . . ." The church also relies on each member's experience of "transcending mystery and wonder," the writings and actions of "prophetic men and women which challenge us to confront powers and structures of evil with justice, compassion, and the transforming power of love," and "[w]isdom from the world's religions."

Also in 1986, the association adopted seven principles calling on members to recognize the worth of each individual and to work for justice, democracy, and free religious expression. With these faith sources and this guiding principle of free searching for life's meaning, Unitarian Universalists are a diverse lot.

Members of the association coming from the former Universalist Church tend to identify themselves as Christians, while adherents joining from the past Unitarian side report a large variety of belief systems. In a poll conducted of Unitarian Universalists during the late 1990s, about forty-six percent said they were humanists, nineteen percent counted themselves as atheists, and another nineteen percent claimed Wicca or another earth- or nature-based religion. About thirteen percent stated they were Christians. Four percent claimed Buddhism, just over one percent said they were Jewish, and small numbers identified themselves as Hindus or Muslims.

As seen from these numbers, humanism represents the largest group within the Unitarian Universalist Association. Today, because of the term *secular humanism,* we tend to think of humanists as non-religious. This view is not entirely correct. Religious humanism was a factor in the Continental and Catholic reformations. John Calvin, leader of the reform church movement, had been trained in humanism, which attempted to bring human-discovered knowledge together with spiritual revelation. During the same time, Erasmus of Rotterdam brought greater rigor to Catholic biblical scholarship through humanist philology, the study of language and literature. Other Catholic humanists were at the forefront of church efforts combating misuse of priestly office and applying reason to church teachings.

Humanism has always placed great importance on reason, freedom, and equality. These attributes are seen as virtues in Unitarian Universalism. Today many humanists reject supernatural guidance for morality, but they do not rebuff morals. Humanists search for morality through a process akin to the scientific method's requirements of observing, hypothesizing, testing, observing again, and using the new information to continue the process. Humanists seek a reasoned moral solution that best meets the needs of the human condition. Sometimes this search arrives at the same body of ethics found through traditional religion.

One of my seminary professors who was a Christian Unitarian Universalist referred to the outcome of the church members' search as "a wonderful anarchy." This anarchy allows local churches to go in their own direction, which means worship services are not consistent throughout the denomination; however, a common element in Unitarian Universalist worship is a chalice lighting. The association's symbol is a shallow chalice holding a flame, and many congregations create that symbol as the beginning of worship. The rest of the service usually includes prayer or meditation, religious readings, hymns and other music, a sermon, and a monetary collection for church ministry and mission.

Church is defined in many ways. It is often referred to as a group of people who come together for worship, doing good, and considering the ultimate questions of life and the universe. Unitarian Universalists meet this definition of the word.

On the Baha'i

I'm often asked whether I make up the questions that appear in "Our Faiths." Because I live in the Bible Belt, where religion is an important topic and people want to discuss it, I don't find that necessary; however, I confess to making up this question. I've never received an inquiry about the Baha'i Faith, but I couldn't write a book on the world's religions without a least mentioning this interesting faith tradition.

Q. What do the Baha'i believe?

A. The Baha'i Faith was founded in Persia, present-day Iran, during the mid-nineteenth century. Although Arabic was not Persia's language, the name Baha'i comes from an Arabic word meaning "glory."

Shortly before his execution in 1850, a Shi'ite Muslim who called himself the *Bab,* meaning "door," predicted the coming of the "Promised One of All Ages." Within a few years, Persian nobleman Mizra Hussein Ali, adopted the name *Baha'u'llah,* meaning "glory for God," and announced he was the promised one.

Baha'u'llah taught all religions worshipped the same God and despite differences in practice and emphasis brought the same message to humankind. He also said God sent various manifestations to the world over the years to progressively reveal God's desires for all people. Among those manifestations were Zoroaster, Abraham, Krishna, Buddha, Moses, Jesus, and Mohammed. Each one dealt with issues in his time and place, but each also brought a message about the oneness of God and the unity of humanity, Baha'u'llah taught.

While the spirit of God dwelled in each of the manifestations, none was God and none was a reincarnation of any other manifestation. For the Baha'i, God is too vast to be fully incorporated in human form. God, in fact, is too complex and at the same time too subtle for human beings to understand completely. The purpose of life, as learned from each of these manifestations is to know and worship God and to live morally, Baha'u'llah said.

The Baha'i Faith teaches each person is responsible for an independent search for truth, and to that end the religion has no clergy. Adherents gather for readings and worship led by the various members of the community. Each believer is also expected to pray daily.

While Baha'u'llah lived in a patriarchal society, he taught men and women are equal in God's eyes; therefore, each gender must be treated the same and have the same rights. The Baha'i work for better health care for women and children and better legal treatment of women in various parts of the world.

As another matter of social action, the Baha'i are dedicated to abolishing both extreme poverty and extreme wealth. They also work for the creation of a universal world language, which is often called an auxiliary language, to improve the chances for world peace and to further the unity of humanity.

On Buddhism

My picture runs with the column, so occasionally someone will recognize me when I'm out. Lisa tapped me on the shoulder in a crowded courthouse elevator and asked this question after telling me how much she enjoyed reading "Our Faiths." I've tried to quote her directly although I didn't have room to write down the question.

Q. How can Buddhism be considered a religion since they are atheists?

—Lisa

A. Buddhism is represented by three major schools—Theravada, found mostly in southeast Asia and Sri Lanka; Mahayana, the most widely practiced form; and Vajrayana, also known as Tibetan Buddhism led by the Dalai Lama. Vajrayana is often classified as a sub group of Mahayana. Most Americans are familiar with Zen Buddhism, which is a Japanese school of Mahayana Buddhism.

The western world often portrays Buddhists as atheists because western theologians do not see God in the form they expect when they look at Buddhism. For Islam, Judaism, and Christianity—the major religions in the West—God is a unique being. He is someone who can be spoken to and perhaps heard from. He has characteristics we can learn and describe. He is someone a believer can have a one-on-one relationship with.

Viewing God in this manner makes for a "personal God." The term does not mean "my own God." Instead, it means a God who has individuality, who exists separately from the universe, and who communicates.

In the various forms of Buddhism, God is not personal. Theravada Buddhism does not speculate on what God is because such speculation is useless in the Theravadan's view. It is a mystery that cannot be known.

In other forms, some believers might ponder the question, but those who seek to answer it do not find a personal God. Instead, they perceive a God who is a force, such as gravity.

Gravity certainly affects the universe, but a human being cannot converse with gravity. Gravity is not embodied, literally or figuratively.

In the same way, for Buddhists who consider the question, God is the force that created the universe and set the great cycle of creation, death, and re-creation into motion. A person cannot communicate with this God.

For a Buddhist, however, the vital questions are not is there a God, who is God, or how do I know God? The vital question has to do with how a person ends suffering. Buddhism believes in reincarnation, but it also teaches life includes suffering. The goal of a believer is to remove himself from the cycle of reincarnation so he will no longer suffer.

Once removed from this cycle, the believer reaches Nirvana. The only way to get out of the cycle is to become enlightened, as the Buddha was enlightened. For Buddhism, the issue is, "How do I become enlightened so that I may reach Nirvana?"

Buddhists identify an eight-fold path to enlightenment. This path requires a person to act, think, and meditate properly. It is the basis of Buddhist morality and the focus of Buddhist spirituality.

In an e-mail, Archie and Louise said they are Baptists who believe each of us should work hard to understand one another and to love one another, regardless of religion. After I answered their question, they wrote a very nice thank you.

Thank you for your article on Buddhism. A question we have: Is Nirvana just a blessed state to be enjoyed here on earth or is it considered to be a blessed state in an eternal dwelling place similar to our New Testament teaching about heaven?

—Archie and Louise

In Sanskrit, the word *nirvana* means blowing out, as in the dousing of a candle. Nirvana refers to the extinguishing of the candle of suffering.

One of the Four Noble Truths of Buddhism holds life is suffering, and the goal of a religious person is to remove himself from the cycle of reincarnation so suffering will end. When an individual removes himself from that cycle, he reaches Nirvana.

In some forms of ancient Hinduism, where the word originated, nirvana was seen as the union of the individual with the universe, so nirvana was not simply a state to be enjoyed on earth. It was the ultimate existence to be enjoyed until the universe no longer existed. It was not a single place, but every place since the universe is everywhere.

For Buddhism, however, Nirvana is somewhat different. In all forms of Buddhism, a goal is to abolish the individual, the "self," so the ancient Hindu belief in a union between the individual and the universe is not accepted.

In Theravada Buddhism, Nirvana comes in two parts. In the first part, a person becomes enlightened as the Buddha was enlightened when he was thirty-five years old. The enlightened person extinguishes the flames of greed and hatred at this time and no longer lives in a state of delusion about the universe. This is a blessed state to be enjoyed here on earth during a person's lifetime.

The second part of Nirvana—sometimes called Parinirvana—comes at the enlightened individual's death and is the ultimate goal to be reached. This is the concept that is most difficult for people to understand. An individual self no longer exists; yet, the person does not become nothingness. Nirvana in this form does not connote a place, as some Christians see heaven, because *place* has no meaning. A Theravada Buddhist says simply this Nirvana cannot be described.

For a Mahayana Buddhist, the goal regarding Nirvana is different. Once again, Nirvana is a state of enlightenment to be enjoyed on earth, but the enlightened person has a different purpose. Rather than seek Parinirvana, an enlightened Mahayana Buddhist becomes a *bodhisattva* (pronounced "bode-dee-sat-vuh.") A bodhisattva is a person who helps other people find enlightenment.

The Nirvana experienced by the bodhisattva is a blessed state enjoyed on earth. Any ultimate Nirvana after death is not considered. What comes will come, what that is cannot be known, and an enlightened individual will automatically realize whatever an existence after life has to offer, in the Mahayana view.

The important thing after earthly enlightenment is to help others to understand. In this way, Mahayana Buddhism is different from its Theravadan cousin. In Theravada Buddhism, no one can help another person obtain enlightenment. In the Mahayana tradition, assisting the whole world to receive enlightenment is the ultimate goal.

Buddhism may be the hardest religion for those of us in the West to understand. Its emphasis on ending physical rebirth seems strange to many of us who do our best to deny death and would prefer to live forever.

Q. How do Buddhists view salvation; in other words, do they think about being saved like Christians do?

—Matt

A. When westerners first encounter Buddhism, they may deem it very pessimistic, but further consideration will show the religion seeks to bring happiness to its adherents.

The Buddha taught there are Four Noble Truths. The first is life continuing suffering. Life will have pain, fear, frustration, and disappointment. The suffering does not cease with death because Buddhism teaches living beings are reincarnated and begin the cycle of suffering again.

The second truth is suffering arises from craving. Individuals constantly want other people to like them. They want material goods to make them comfortable. They desire power.

The third truth teaches suffering can be overcome and happiness can be attained when craving is abolished from a person's life.

The fourth truth says craving can be defeated and suffering ended by following the Noble Eight-fold Path. By following this path, an individual can become enlightened or awakened. "Buddha," in fact, comes from a word meaning "awaken."

The enlightened individual is removed from the cycle of reincarnation at death and experiences Nirvana or, in some schools of Buddhism,

Parinirvana. Each is a state that cannot be adequately described, but each offers freedom from suffering.

The Eight-fold Path seeks to bring morality and focus to life. The first portion of this path is to have the "right view," which consists of accepting Buddhist teachings until a person can experience the teachings' truth for himself.

The second part is to develop "right resolve" by committing to religious study so proper attitudes can be adopted. The third portion is to use only "right speech," meaning telling the truth and speaking thoughtfully.

The fourth element is "right action," which is typically stated in the negative: A believer abstains from wrong behavior, such as killing and stealing. The fifth component calls for the believer to engage in "right livelihood." The adherent's occupation cannot be one that brings harm to any other person.

The sixth part requires adherents to embrace "right effort," meaning they must control their thoughts and cultivate positive mental states. The seventh portion requires "right mindfulness," which means believers must be constantly aware of themselves, the cosmos, and wisdom.

The final component is "right meditation." This piece of the path is considered essential for all other parts. A Buddhist seeks to develop physical, emotional, intellectual, and spiritual calm so the mind can be fully awakened to the enlightenment of Nirvana.

So the answer to the question is yes, Buddhists ponder salvation. For them it is a matter of rescue from life and removal from the requirement to live physically again and again.

This question came from one of my editors who attended various Zen Buddhist talks and meditation sessions.

We may have differing perspectives on Buddhism. It's really more of a question of emphasis than anything else. You seem to focus on suffering in Buddhism, but I understand it as a pathway to inner peace and tranquility.

—Shauna

A. Suffering is the human condition recognized in the Four Noble Truths as laid out by the Buddha; however, these truths are not offered as a lament for human life; instead, they present hope. The third noble truth says suffering can be overcome, and the fourth truth explains how.

As explained by the Dalai Lama, leader of the Vajrayana school of Buddhism, people can attempt to overcome suffering in this physical life and in the existence to come by external or internal means.

External means include amassing wealth, acquiring power, and obtaining food and shelter, among other things. After reaching these goals, most people find they still suffer because they want even more and because they have not escaped the *samsara* cycle of birth-death-reincarnation.

In Judeo-Christian terms, even the most successful individuals find themselves wondering, "Is this all there is?" in same manner as the teacher in the Book of Ecclesiastes who finally decides life is "vanity of vanities," as the King James Version puts it.

Buddhism focuses on internal means of finding peace. The Dalai Lama teaches people must develop morality, wisdom, and concentrated meditation to discover calmness and tranquility.

Buddhist morality contends a person should take action to help others, or he should at least act in a way that harms no one else. Morality arises from a person constantly questioning his motivation for actions and desires. By questioning the motivation for the time in which a person wants something or desires an action to be completed, he develops patience.

To prepare for proper meditation, a Buddhist practices patience throughout the day. While there are many forms of meditation, the practice known as "calm abiding" or "stabilizing meditation" brings the tranquility many seek. The Dalai Lama teaches a person who wishes to meditate needs to set a specific time and find a quiet place for her stabilizing efforts. She should be rested and properly fed and assume a comfortable position that is not so relaxing she can fall asleep.

The individual also needs to find an object to concentrate on for meditation. Many concentrate on their breath. Others focus on the first letter of their names or a mantra such as the word *aum*. Still others picture the Buddha, or if they are not Buddhist, another religious figure. The person meditating attempts to keep all other thoughts out of her mind.

After practice, calm abiding meditation brings tranquility and relaxation, allowing an individual to deal with the stresses of life. Success in overcoming stress increases morality as the adherent more successfully considers his motivations.

Success in concentrated meditation also brings a believer to the point where she can develop wisdom. In Buddhism, wisdom begins with understanding human beings operate under delusions about life and existence. Those delusions are too extensive to deal with completely in this short space, but in a nutshell, Buddhism teaches appearance is not reality.

In Buddhist thought, wisdom requires reasoning, and reasoning involves focusing the mind through meditation. We can comprehend Buddhist reasoning by looking at the first part of the Noble Eight-fold Path. This portion requires "right view," which means accepting Buddhist teachings until a person can experience their truth for herself. To do this, the adherent listens to a teacher. After understanding the teacher, she searches the words of doctrine for herself. She concentrates on all the true meanings of the words to eventually discover the definitive meaning. While looking for that definitive meaning, she avoids applying simple, dualistic understandings, choosing instead to consider the possibilities that all are correct, none are right, all are partially true, some are more accurate than others, and so forth.

The goal at the end of the entire process is to bring peace to a person's life and freedom from future suffering.

On Taoism

Mike is an attorney and former judge who loves to discuss religious and philosophical issues. He wanted the column to branch out from what he considered "the same old stuff."

Q. You've talked mostly about Islam and Christianity. You haven't mentioned any Eastern religions. I'd like to know about them, especially Taoism.

—Mike

A. Taoism (pronounced "dow-ism") is an ancient Chinese belief system with four basic expressions. It can be practiced as a religion, philosophy, health regimen, or any combination of these three.

Philosophical Taoism traces its origin to the chaotic Chinese "Warring States" era of the fourth century B.C.E., when a short volume called *Tao Te Ching,* meaning "The Classic Book of the Way and Its Power," appeared. Proponents said the book was written by a Sixth Century B.C.E. philosopher known as Lao Tzu, "the grand old master."

Philosophical Taoism teaches Tao, "the Way," is an indescribable natural force that moves and unites the world. People created personal dissatisfaction, social breakdown, and political anarchy by attempting to impose their inferior knowledge on life instead of allowing the Way to control.

By becoming humble, acting in moderation, and exercising compassion, adherents can allow Tao's energetic flow to bring them and their society happiness.

Proper direction of this energetic flow to protect health and obtain longevity is the object of "vitalizing Taoism," what the West might call a health regimen. Chinese medicinal practices involving acupuncture and herbal remedies, as well as deliberate movement such as found in Tai Chi, are part of vitalizing Taoism.

Religious Taoism concerns itself with restoring proper equilibrium to individual lives and the world as a whole by balancing *yin* and *yang,* which are the two aspects of life-giving energy. *Yin* is feminine, shady, and cool. *Yang* is male, sunny, and warm. Each is required for anyone to attain harmony with Tao.

Religious Taoism finds expression in what may be called a priestly form and a popular form. In the priestly form, Tao is the creative force of the universe. In the West, we call this force God.

In the priestly form of Taoism, however, Tao is not a personal god. A personal God, such as the God of Judaism or Christianity, is a distinct being with whom believers can have a relationship. In the West, the Supreme Being can be talked to and listened to. God knows us, and we can know God, though imperfectly.

In priestly Taoism, no personal relationship is possible with Tao. Instead of having a being, Tao is a force, as gravity and electromagnetism are forces. Tao is the ultimate force and can be relied upon to act in certain ways, but it cannot be known.

Popular Taoism introduces various personal gods to this religious system. Among them is Lao Tzu, the founder of Taoism, who is understood to have become a god after "traveling to the West." In Chinese literature, "traveling to the West," is a euphemism for dying. In ancient days, heaven was seen as lying somewhere west of China.

Popular Taoism understands heaven is operated like a government or business bureaucracy, with various gods responsible for different aspects of the universe. The Jade Emperor serves as heaven's administrator and is in charge of all physical and spiritual existence, but he is not all-powerful. Lao Tzu is greater, and the Heavenly Sage is greater still.

The Heavenly Sage is the original being and as close to a personification of Tao as any form of Taoism comes.

Popular Taoism teaches life and the universe will someday cease, but Tao will recreate both. Just as he has done in past creations, the Heavenly Sage will explain Tao to the world when the universe is renewed.

Other gods include the Ten Kings of the Hells and the Three Gods of Happiness. During the Chinese New Year and at funerals, Taoists burn colorful paper money bearing the portrait of King Yama, one of the Ten Kings of the Hells, as a way of bribing the gods for better treatment of believers' ancestors.

The most important of the Three Gods of Happiness is the god of immortality. Attainment of immortality has been the major focus of traditional Chinese medicine, based on the principles of Taoism, for centuries.

Taoism was one of the three great religions in China, along with Buddhism and Confucianism, but fell out of official favor in 1911 with the demise of the Ch'ing Dynasty. The triumph of Maoist communism in 1949 and its decade-long Cultural Revolution starting in the 1960s further eroded Taoist practices.

Today, Taoism's strongholds are in Hong Kong and on Taiwan, although New Age religions in the West have begun to incorporate some of the teachings.

On Hinduism

Over the years, different practices have been criticized as anti-Christian. A vocal group has fought Halloween as a glorification of paganism and Christmas for being celebrated during an ancient Roman holiday. Gwen's e-mail indicated her parents were concerned her exercise regimen would convert her from Christianity.

Q. After many years of being out of shape, I've finally found something that helps me. It's yoga, but my parents (I don't live at home) are furious because they think I'm being taken over by a cult. Can you help me explain to them yoga is not religious?

—GWEN

A. The techniques and philosophy of yoga come from Hinduism, the name westerners have given the religion practiced in India since ancient times. A person who engages in yoga is known as a yogi, and a yogi has a variety of forms of yoga to choose from. There are tremendous differences in the forms practiced by devout Hindus and those used by many westerners as a physical exercise. Generally yoga requires a yogi to adopt physical postures, control breathing, withdraw from consideration of the five senses, concentrate, meditate, and contemplate.

In the United States and other parts of the West, the most popular form of yoga is called hatha yoga. As practiced in America, it emphasizes physical postures, controlled breathing, meditation, and chakras—energy centers in the body. Its goals often are development of patience, improved health, weight loss, and blood pressure control.

Many Hindu yogis complain western-style hatha yoga has divorced the spiritual component of the practice from the physical. Generally yoga's goal is to develop self-mastery and to unite all of a person's parts—physical, spiritual and mental—into an effective, powerful whole. Many believe that through yoga a person can assure the attachment of good karma to her soul, allowing the yogi to enter Moeksha at death. Moeksha is a state of blissful existence in which the soul is released from the cycle of reincarnation. Some Hindus avoid the term Moeksha and prefer to call this existence "unity with God."

For the one billion Hindus in the world, yoga is divided into five or perhaps six general types. Hatha yoga is practiced with a more spiritual aim than usually found in the West. Bhakti yoga is also known as the "path of love" or the "path of devotion." It seeks to create calmness and attitudes of service and friendship.

Karma yoga may also be called the "path of action." It strives to control a yogi's motivations so they are pure and lead to good and helpful actions. Raja yoga is also known as the "royal path." It brings a scientific approach to yoga and places tremendous importance on focusing energy.

Jnana yoga also bears the name "path of knowledge." This form attempts to find enlightenment by concentrating on the question "Who am I?" A relatively new form is called integral yoga, founded in the mid-twentieth century. It combines the various other schools of thought on yoga into one so-called integrated approach.

While Hindus applying one of yoga's forms insist religious insight should be sought and Hindu principles applied to a person's life, many western practitioners see yoga as simply a form of exercise and relaxation that does not require acceptance of any new or different faith traditions.

Of the five largest faith traditions in the world's religions, Hinduism is unique in that it has a huge number of adherents but is mostly confined to a small geographic arena. It is the opposite in this way of Judaism, a faith with the smallest number of believers among the so-called Big Five, but present in almost every corner of the world. Because the vast majority of it's practitioners live in India, Hinduism remains a mystery to many Americans.

Q. I have always understood Hinduism to be a polytheistic religion, but I was told recently that it's monotheistic. Is this true, and if so, how can it be? I don't think it is with all the gods they worship.

—Tina

A. It has been said there are as many forms of Hinduism as there are villages in India. It is difficult to generalize about Hinduism, but we may look for answers in some modern understandings of this ancient faith—perhaps the oldest continuously practiced religion in the world.

Hinduism is the name the West has given a religious tradition that evolved slowly over the past five or more millennia on the Asian Subcontinent, today's India, Pakistan, and Bangladesh. It appears to combine faith practices from European Aryans, believed to have migrated to India some five thousand years ago, and indigenous traditions of that time, with later developments to create a new faith system.

With some three hundred million gods said to inhabit the Hindu pantheon, an observer could easily believe Hinduism is a polytheistic faith. Some Hindus in those scattered Indian villages may say it is. Other adherents, however, point to various Vedas and Upanishads, Sanskrit scriptures expressing Hinduism's history and beliefs, to show the faith worships one true God. As an example, the *Great Aranyaka Upanishad* records a conversation between Guru Yajnavalkya and a questioner: "'Yajnavalkya, how many gods are there?' 'One,' [Yajnavalkya answered]. 'Yes, of course,' [the questioner] said, 'but then who are those three and three hundred, and those three and three thousand?' 'They are only the powers of the god,' Yajnavalkya replied," *Great Aranyaka Upanishad* 3.9.1-2. Another Upanishad states, "He is the one God, hidden in all beings, all-pervading, the Self within all beings, watching over all works, dwelling in all beings, the witness, the perceiver, the only one, free from qualities," *Svetasvatara Upanishad* 6.11.

In all religions, scholarly theology sometimes is lost in the day-to-day activities of the faith's practitioners. This loss may also occur in Hinduism; however, Hindu gurus generally teach that Brahman is the one Supreme Being, Primal Soul, and Ultimate Reality. Aspects of Brahman are known to the world through the Hindu Trinity of Brahma, creator of the universe; Vishnu, preserver of the universe; and Shiva, destroyer of the universe. This Trinity is also understood as truth, love, and bliss. As with the Christian Trinity, each aspect of the Hindu Trinity is separate but at the same time each is merely a part of the ultimate God.

Christianity teaches Christ, the second person of the Christian Trinity, was incarnated in human flesh. The persons of the Hindu Trinity, likewise, took human and other animal forms. In Hinduism's case, however, all three aspects of the Trinity became manifest and each assumed physical existence many times. These manifestations are known as *avatars,* and the most famous to the West is Krishna, an avatar of Vishnu. Krishna is considered the embodiment of divine love, much as Jesus is perceived in Christianity.

In addition, Hindus view each attribute and power of the Supreme Being as a different god or goddess. Ascribing these attributes and powers to various gods is believed to make divinity and the workings of the universe easier to comprehend. The creation of these many minor deities expresses Hinduism's understanding that God is everywhere and God's power is in all things: "The Supreme Being is thousand-headed, thousand-eyed, thousand-footed; and, pervading the earth on all sides, He exists beyond the ten directions, " Rig Veda 10.90.1.

Acting through Brahma, Brahman created the universe with its karmic law of cause and effect. Every action has a consequence or reaction, good or bad. As any living being progresses through life, these reactions, or karmas, attach to his soul, or *atman.* The weight of good and bad karma will determine an individual's reincarnated status after physical death. Someone with an abundance of bad karma will be reincarnated into a lesser life, perhaps even an animal's life. A person with more good karma will find new life in a higher status. In Hindu understanding, Brahman has created a system requiring birth, death, and rebirth until an individual atman obtains enough good karma to be released from the cycle. At that release, the atman merges with the Primal Soul in a blissful condition known as Moeksha, or unity with God.

Finally, if a Christian was asked to summarize God in one word, he would probably use the word *love.* If a Hindu was asked to do the same thing, she would choose *truth.* Hinduism is concerned with uncovering the truths of the universe: how it operates and how that operation affects an individual's life and reincarnation to come, as well as how it can release a fortunate person from the cycle of rebirth so she may find happiness in Moeksha.

On the Hmong

With the 1975 fall of Saigon, huge numbers of Southeast Asian refugees immigrated to the United States. Many of these individuals were housed at Fort Chafee near the Oklahoma-Arkansas border until they could find permanent homes. A large number of these refugees settled in Oklahoma City and changed the religious landscape. Not only was Buddhism introduced, but also various tribal religions.

Q. I would like to ask you a question about the Hmong religion. I am not a member but I have a relative who is employed by these people and am curious. I know the people are from Laos and most of them are of the Hmong religion, but that's all I know.

—Marilyn

A. Many Hmong came to the United States following the American withdrawal from Southeast Asia and the subsequent fall of South Vietnam. The Hmong were among America's fiercest allies and soldiers in the Central Intelligence Agency's "secret army" seeking to close the Ho Chi Minh Trail through countries neighboring Vietnam.

The Hmong probably originated in Siberia and made their way to southern China almost five thousand years ago before moving to Southeast Asia. Siberia was the seat of a shamanistic religion, and the religious practices of the Hmong exhibit both shamanism and animism.

Shamanism is a religious system in which a shaman—also known in the West as a medicine man—serves as a medium between the spirit and physical worlds. The shaman normally helps other individuals communicate with spirits, including the spirits of deceased ancestors.

Animism is a religious system in which adherents understand that most things in the physical world have spirits or souls. A spirit is said to animate the object. The spirits are believed to cause natural and supernatural phenomena to occur.

Among traditional Hmong following the group's ancient religious beliefs, the spirit world is understood to include ancestor spirits, house spirits, and nature spirits. If spirits become offended by a lack of attention or by improper actions in a Hmong family or community, the souls may cause illness or catastrophe to befall an individual. Many Hmong rituals, therefore, are directed toward appeasing these spirits. Such rituals include animal sacrifice and the playing of a special reed pipe, called the *qeej*.

Occasionally evil spirits will cause harm in a community for no reason, and special rituals must be performed to end a curse or other problem. The unpredictability of these evil spirits is one reason that Hmong do not like anyone to praise their children—for example, by calling a baby "pretty"—because they fear an evil spirit may hear the praise and focus a vile deed on the child.

The Hmong believe each person has twelve souls, and one of the common acts perpetrated by evil spirits is to steal one of these souls. A person missing one of the twelve souls will be ill.

In the Hmong religion, which has no separate name since the religion is part and parcel of the culture, adherents believe in reincarnation. Upon physical death, a person's souls will attempt to find their way to the "land of darkness" where they will be prepared for rebirth.

To assist the souls in this travel, traditional Hmong bury a child's placenta, known as the "birth shirt," at the birthplace. A boy's placenta will be buried under a main post of the home, and a girl's will be buried under the parents' bed.

On Scientology

Tom is from "Little Dixie" in southeast Oklahoma. His interest in Scientology was spurred when Tom Cruise made a splash on television talking about his Scientology-based dislike of drugs.

Q. What is the Church of Scientology that TV and movie actors are so into?

—Tom

A. Scientology resulted from the writings of science fiction author L. Ron Hubbard, who died in 1986. The word, coined by Hubbard, means "knowing about knowing" or "study of truth."

Scientology seeks to bring scientific methods to the practice of religion. To that end, the Church of Scientology teaches no one is required to accept any concept by faith; instead, adherents are said to believe only what they observe.

Scientology teaches humans are spiritual as well as physical and mental beings. That spiritual being is known as the "thetan." A person's thetan is believed to have inhabited various physical bodies in the past and to be capable of existing independently from any body.

The thetan is basically good, but human beings have lost the ability to communicate with this thetan at the core of their existence because of static or interference that has collected over time, according to Scientology's theology. Many of life's difficulties are caused by this static; therefore, a goal of the church is to help individuals achieve a greater degree of spiritual awareness by removing the interference.

While the Church of Scientology conducts weekly services in which a sermon is given, the central work of the group comes in "auditing sessions" where a member attempts to clear the interference blocking the thetan. An "auditor" uses an "electropsychometer," more commonly called an "E-meter," to help the member, known in the session as a "preclear," deal with an "upset" causing spiritual disability. An upset may be any thought, emotion, reaction or similar phenomenon preventing an individual from using all his spiritual abilities. The goal of the session is to increase a person's ability to deal with life through the thetan.

The E-meter is an instrument said to be capable of measuring the activity of the mind and its connection to the thetan. The meter consists of a box with a needle that moves along a scale, a few knobs and two electrodes on wires. The preclear holds the electrodes while the auditor asks questions to find the upset.

Once an upset is discovered, the auditor asks additional questions or gives directions intended to discharge the upset, as shown by the needle on the meter. Some people have dubbed auditing sessions as "meditation through science."

Because of Scientology's emphasis on developing a clear mind with the ability to communicate with the thetan, the church strongly opposes the use of mind-altering drugs, whether legal or illegal. This opposition extends to the use of anesthesia when such pain-killing drugs are thought unnecessary.

Scientology also criticizes the practice of psychiatry because of doctors' reliance on drugs to treat patients and because the church believes psychiatry and psychology teach human beings are merely animals and not spiritual beings.

Post Script: *Narconon is the drug rehabilitation arm of the Church of Scientology. In the late 1980s, a Narconon program was established in northern Oklahoma Indian country.*

On the Urantia Brotherhood

The Urantia Brotherhood is among the newest of religious expressions and little known to most of the world. The Urantia Book, *basic scripture for the group, has sold more than two hundred fifty thousand copies worldwide and is being translated into a host of languages.*

Q. I met someone recently who was introduced to me as a member of a brotherhood that I can't spell but sounded like "your rancha." I took it from our conversation that this is a religion. Do you know what it is?

—Gene

A. You are probably speaking of the Urantia Brotherhood.

In the 1920s, a woman brought her husband to Dr. William Sadler, a psychiatrist on the University of Chicago medical school faculty and also a lecturer in pastoral counseling at McCormick Theological Seminary. The husband talked incessantly in his sleep about immortal beings who had created earth and were trying to improve it.

When awake, the man remembered nothing of what he said and exhibited no interest in the topic. Over the next ten years or so, Sadler recorded the patient's sleeping monologue and eventually produced the *Urantia Book,* a twenty-one hundred-page tome, from the recordings.

The *Urantia Book* explains the world we know as Earth is called Urantia by the beings who created it. They have generated thousands of life-containing planets in this universe.

Creation on Earth has not developed as planned because of failings on the part of individuals sent to the planet to cultivate it, including Adam and Eve, according to the Urantia Foundation, which publishes the book.

The revelation of the *Urantia Book* is the latest attempt to set the creation back on track. The last such effort was the visit of a special being known to humanity as Jesus Christ, according to the Urantia Brotherhood.

The brotherhood, established as a church in 1950, teaches God exists at the center of a universe of made up of eight smaller universes, Christ is God's son, and Lucifer and Satan are immortal beings who rebelled against God in an attempt to take control of Urantia's universe.

Each person has the free will to accept God's love and way of life or to reject it. Those who accept have the opportunity to receive a "morontia" body after death, which is a physical body that does not require food or other inputs to survive.

The Urantia Brotherhood does not conduct worship services or construct church buildings. Instead, it seeks to further knowledge of its beliefs through discussion groups online and in person—including some church-based groups. Each person is expected to continue to worship in his own faith tradition and to bring Urantia concepts to those traditions.

On Satanism

This article elicited a response from someone calling himself "Modesto," an avowed Satanist. He wanted me to know the Church of Satan does not include the first two groups I write about below in their definition of Satanists, but he agreed with what I said about his church.

Q. You said you won't attack any religion in your column, but I bet that doesn't apply to my religion: Satanism.

—NO NAME GIVEN

A. An absence of criticism should never be misunderstood as agreement. This column seeks to inform rather than to judge.

Satanism comes in three major forms. In Middle America, the most prevalent practitioners are white, middle-class, teenage boys who have a psychological need to rebel against their parents. Research indicates these boys rarely join a satanic group, and their limited doctrine is founded predominantly on their desire to cast aside their parents' values for a time.

Another major group of satanic practitioners consists of sociopaths who have entered a world of crime or will soon do so. Faced with the reality of their bad behavior and unable to accept responsibility for their choices, these people decide they are possessed by devilish forces. They surrender to this thought and worship Satan. Again, studies have found these adherents typically do not join groups of like-minded people but develop beliefs in a haphazard manner that fits their purposes at any given moment.

Neither of these first two forms finds expression in an orderly body; however, the third form of Satanism consists of organized churches found mostly on the West Coast.

Organized satanic churches do not actually worship Satan. They worship pleasure. The first of these groups in America was founded by photographer and organist Anton LaVey in San Francisco in the mid-1960s. He chose the name Church of Satan to garner attention and to announce his opposition to various Christian concepts such as forgiveness and sin.

The Church of Satan is founded on the philosophy of hedonism. Anything that is pleasurable should be allowed, LaVey said in his 1969 book, *The Satanic Bible.*

The Church of Satan teaches avarice is a good human emotion leading to progress. Lust should be indulged by men and women; otherwise, they become unhealthy, LaVey said. "Satan represents all of the so-called sins, as they all lead to physical, mental, or emotional gratification," LaVey wrote in his "Nine Satanic Statements," which summarize the group's beliefs.

Pleasure is the rule. As LaVey put it, "Satan represents indulgence, instead of abstinence."

Contrary to popular belief, the Church of Satan and its offshoots do not practice animal sacrifice and certainly do not entertain human sacrifice. LaVey contended people who believed that any animal or human's life force could be obtained through blood sacrifice misunderstood the power of magic. The life force, he said, was best released through discharges of biological energy involved in strong emotions, such as "blind anger, mortal terror, or consuming grief."

Various other satanic churches have split from the Church of Satan, the largest believed to be the Temple of Set, which worships the ancient Egyptian god Seti, who provided pleasure to people.

While hedonism is the byword in these churches, they uniformly oppose harming other people because of the religion's belief no one should prevent another person from experiencing pleasure.

Involving Death

It turns out that Katy is actually a dog, and this question was sent by her owner.

Q. My minister said pets don't go to heaven, only people. Do any religions believe pets go to heaven, too?

—KATY

A. Most popular concepts about the afterlife, Heaven, and Hell are not scriptural. Instead, many of our thoughts about such things come from poems, novels, and the movies.

In the West, for example, Dante's "Inferno" has had a powerful effect on what Europeans and Americans believe about Hell. The films *Heaven Can Wait* and *Here Comes Mr. Jordan* and even Bugs Bunny cartoons have had a greater impact on American ideas about Heaven than any religion's scripture.

The primary reason for this is the Hebrew Bible, Christian Bible, and Muslim Qur'an don't contain a great deal of detailed information about human afterlife. Each of these scriptures is more concerned with instructing men and women on matters important to salvation and living this current life appropriately. Information is even sparser on animals.

This is not to say, these holy books are unconcerned with animals. Each teaches God created all animals, as well as human beings. Each teaches the lives of animals are sacred.

Recognizing meat as an important food source, each of these scriptures lays down definite rules to preserve the sanctity of animal life even in the process of death. The many rules about sacrifices and about what meat can or cannot be eaten seek to remind believers all life is precious.

But these scriptures are silent about the exact nature of animal existence and whether our pets enjoy an afterlife. The best answer to be gleaned from the written word of these religions about whether pets go to Heaven is, we don't know.

For the major eastern religions, the answer is different. Buddhism and Hinduism believe in reincarnation. These religions teach when a life ends—whether human or animal—the creature is reborn.

How the creature is reborn depends on the karma attached to its soul during its previous life. An animal with a profusion of good karma will be reborn as a person. A person with good karma will be reborn to a better status in human life.

This belief in reincarnation serves as the foundation for Hindu vegetarianism. In Hinduism, this cycle of reincarnation continues until the appropriate amount of good karma is attached to a soul so the person reaches *Moeksha*, a heavenly existence, also known as unity with God. It appears animals may eventually reach this blessed plane but only after going through a human existence.

In Buddhism, the reincarnation cycle continues until a person becomes enlightened and attains Nirvana, an unexplainable state beyond this world. Generally, enlightenment requires understanding beyond animal capability; however, as with Hinduism, an animal may reach this state by going through a reincarnated existence as a human being. It should be pointed out, however, Buddhism teaches that one of the many previous Buddhas reached enlightenment from a turtle's existence.

Traditional Native American religions, Japanese Shintoism, and traditional African religions, such as that of the Yoruba, believe in spiritual worlds populated by the spirits of both humans and animals. For these faiths, connected more intimately with the natural world than others, it is believed cats, dogs, parakeets, and other animals enter the afterlife just as people do.

Post Script: After this column appeared, some readers complained that I hadn't expressed my own opinion about whether pets enjoy an afterlife. Scripture tells us that God values all life in the creation, so I believe even animals can go to Heaven—but I have to admit that's based on my feelings for my cats, rather than deep theological considerations.

As a pastor, I have heard from people who are upset by viewing a deceased person in the casket. It's important to remember no one is required to view the body. In funerals where a viewing takes place, when the ushers bring out the mourners on your row, simply walk to the back of the church rather than following the row to the front where the casket is. Viewing is an individual choice.

Q. We moved here a few years ago from Ohio. We've been surprised by Oklahoma funerals where the deceased is in full view of the people. Caskets were never open in Ohio. Why do Oklahomans open them?

—Jackie

A. Funeral practices vary greatly from faith to faith and place to place.

In the Jewish community, burial occurs as soon as possible and without embalming the body. Jews do not view a deceased person's remains, believing such observation is disrespectful.

In the orthodox Hindu community, however, mourners view the dead person's face. After the body is washed by family members, it is placed on a stretcher and covered with flowers, framing but not concealing the face, which remains uncovered until cremation. Normally, the body is cremated within twenty-four hours of death and preferably not more than three days later.

Among the Muslim faithful, a family member also washes the body but then wraps the entire corpse in one or more *kafan* or coffin cloths, usually made of cotton. Traditional Islamic practice calls for burying the deceased in the *kafan,* without a Western-style casket, as soon as possible.

Baha'is follow a similar body-cleansing practice, with the job of washing the corpse considered a great honor. Typically, the family wraps a silk shroud around the remains and places the body in a wooden or stone casket. According to Baha'u'llah, the Baha'i prophet, "the sooner burial takes place, the more fitting and preferable."

In Buddhist society, the coffin remains open during funeral services so mourners may view the deceased and bow to the body as a final sign of respect. The time of cremation usually depends on the dead person's cultural background.

Among Christians, many practices take place. Unlike other faiths, Christianity does not insist on speedy burial or cremation. The later the funeral, the more likely that the body will be embalmed.

Some Roman Catholics conduct a one- to three-day wake before the funeral. The open coffin is present, and mourners view the body as a way of saying goodbye. At the end of the wake, the casket is closed and not reopened.

Many Protestant denominations avoid wakes, but open the coffin at the end of the funeral service. Mourners may file past the corpse as they leave the sanctuary or funeral home to offer their final respects to the dead. Individuals choose to view the body or not, depending on their own preferences.

Other Protestant denominations keep the coffin closed throughout the service. Viewing is expected to take place at the funeral home prior to the funeral. These Protestant groups believe the funeral should emphasize the coming resurrection of the dead. Looking at the body is thought to take the focus off the Christian message of hope.

In the Orthodox Christian tradition, coffins typically remain open during the funeral service, and mourners may kiss the head as a final good-bye.

Before the middle of the twentieth century, most Americans died at home. Death was experienced by the survivors. An ecumenical group of clergy and psychologists today believe the grieving process has been harmed by allowing—some would say, requiring—individuals to die in hospitals and nursing homes, out of the family's view.

Family members naturally want to deny death has occurred; yet, it is thought survivors cannot begin mourning until they remove from their minds the possibility the deceased family member will soon return home. Open caskets, either at the funeral itself, at a wake, or in the viewing room of a funeral home, cause us to confront death in a manner that closed coffins deny. This practice also requires us to recognize the finitude of our own lives. Among those who prefer open caskets, the hope is that such confrontation will cause us to question how we live and to make changes for the better.

Rick is a minister who moved to Oklahoma from the southeastern United States. He wanted to know about what he saw as a curious practice in his new state.

Q. This thought comes from reading your article on funeral practices. I'm a Presbyterian minister. My interest is the number of funerals here where the cemetery burial is first. There's usually a private, family time at the cemetery then we return to the church where the congregation is gathered to worship God and give God thanks for the life of this person. I would say that upwards of about fifty percent of the funerals I participate in are done this way. I would welcome any thoughts and experiences you might have in this area.

—Rick

A. An increasing number of Christian families are opting for private burial followed by a public ritual at church, the funeral home, or even a private home. As you know, when the body of the deceased person is not present at the ceremony, the worship experience is known as a memorial service.

Conflicting issues seem to be at play in this trend toward more private funerals followed by public memorial services. Since the successes of the women's liberation movement from the 1960s onward, men have benefited from new freedom to express tender emotions more openly. In seminary grief counseling classes, pastors-in-training learn it is helpful for men to release emotions—especially those surrounding the mourning process—through tears. But many men remain uncomfortable with such public expressions.

At the same time, women fighting for their rightful place in the business world and society in general are told to control their emotions more tightly than the past's stereotype of a weak female if they wish to be taken seriously. (In some cultures, this stereotype persists and women may be prohibited by social mores from attending a funeral because of what the male-dominated culture perceives as unseemly "wailing.")

Neither men nor women appear entirely comfortable with these relatively new changes. A private memorial service gives both sexes the opportunity to express their grief without fear of appearing weak publicly.

Among parishioners I have helped through the mourning process, the thought is the catharsis of a private funeral will allow each mourner to control his or her emotions in public and avoid embarrassment.

At the same time, a growing number of Protestant churches have changed the public service from a time of mourning to a time of rejoicing for the deceased individual's time on earth. Obituaries often announce a "celebration of life" rather than a funeral.

Other churches have renamed services surrounding death as a "home going." The expectation seems to be that survivors should be pleased their family member or friend has gone to be with God.

In either case, families may feel that full expression of their grief is inappropriate. After all, how can one be sad a loved one has found her way to heaven? Isn't it disrespectful to weep during a celebration?

Despite the societal statement that expressing emotion is okay and even healthy, American society at the same time—including many churches—seems to want to take away a person's ability and right to grieve. Witnessing true mourning prevents us from denying the power of death, and we would rather not acknowledge that power.

This shift appears currently to be a European-American trend and often confined to Christianity. Judaism, for example, expects mourning and has institutionalized a process that gives full permission to grieving.

Christians, intent on giving thanks for God's gift of salvation, may have forgotten that even Jesus mourned publicly when he learned his friend Lazarus had died, as portrayed so straightforwardly in the New Testament's shortest verse, "Jesus wept," John 11:35. Proper mourning allows a family to deal with strong emotions surrounding the loss of an important person, but it also allows all of us to deal with our own fear of death. For that reason, the move to entirely private funerals appears unhealthy.

Postlude

I wrote the following column not for "Our Faiths," but as the weekly exhortation in our local church newsletter. While it's directed to my own United Methodist congregation, it applies to each of the large proselytizing religions—Islam, Buddhism, and Christianity—as well as to all believers who want their faith traditions to be understood.

During the 1970s, I was a journalist—first as a sports writer for our hometown newspaper and later as police reporter for *The Daily Oklahoman.* Thirty years later, I returned to the pages of the *Oklahoman* with a fortnightly column called "Our Faiths." The column seeks to help people of various religions and denominations understand one another.

Times have really changed in the newspaper business since the Seventies. In those days, we reporters thought we had moved up a step when we exchanged our manual, key-jamming Royal typewriters for purring IBM Selectrics with a ball-like typing element.

We had no idea of the changes to come. Today, I write my column at home, instead of in the newsroom. I use a word-processing program on my Gateway computer that automatically checks for spelling and grammar errors, and I submit my words over the Internet to editors I never see.

The Internet has also changed interaction with readers. I still remember the single letter I received during the entire Seventies from a subscriber who read one of my stories. Today, dozens of readers e-mail their electronic jottings within moments of seeing the column.

These spontaneous notes have surprised me. Some are complimentary, some disagree. Others ask new questions, spurred by the earlier column. Quite a few contain a vitriol that baffles me.

I am not an ingénue staggered by the rawness of people's emotions and baser instincts. I have, after all, reported on murders, kidnappings, and worse. I am an assistant district attorney in my "day job," witnessing daily the cruelty and deceit human beings are willing to visit on one another.

No, the harshness confounds me because of who it comes from. Each of these vitriolic writers, except one, has been a person who proclaims himself or herself a Christian. The one exception—the one person who joins these self-described Christians in hate-filled writing—calls himself an atheist.

I have yet to receive an e-mail, letter, or telephone call from a Jew, Muslim, Hindu, Buddhist, Baha'i, Wiccan, or other faith member whose words approach the utter disdain Christians and this one atheist have demonstrated for people of other traditions—not even from the two self-described Satanists who have written.

Usually these writers, after listing their impeccable Christian credentials, demand I inform the correspondents to my column they are doomed to Hell because they hold the wrong faith. This lost group includes, by the way, Mormons, Roman Catholics, and even United Methodists, according to these writers.

Typically, these critics also want to declare their American patriotism; their support of the Founding Fathers, who came here to escape religious persecution; and their desire to have the First Amendment protect them from "vile," "devil-driven," "baby-killing" religions.

I don't agree with every religion I write about. I consciously chose to be a Christian because of God's grace bestowed on me, and I yearn for the day when the truth of God's love for humanity, as contained in the example of Christ, is recognized by all people. I consciously chose to be a United Methodist because of the denomination's message of hope and its recognition of the value of every human being.

I have learned over almost a dozen years of ministry harsh words do not convert. Wrath does not entice worshippers inside our doors. Closed minds cannot hear what is being said so that we might respond to the concerns that seekers bring with them.

Individuals we speak with want to be treated with respect. They want to be treated lovingly. They do not respond well to threats of damnation—however well-intentioned.

As a sixteen-year-old high school student, I was searching for a faith home because I was unhappy with the Roman Catholic Church where I was raised. During this time, my algebra teacher took me into the hall after I had finished a test and told me he understood I was Catholic. He wanted to me to know I was doomed to eternal punishment because I was not a member of the true church. The true church happened to be his. Despite my searching for a new spiritual home, I refused to attend his church or any other in his denomination because I did not like being treated that way.

How can Christians of any stripe expect people to come to the faith or to a denomination within that faith with such belittling and hateful "evangelism"? In a truly oxymoronic way, the hate is well-intentioned. Despite the loathing, the message is munificent, but good intentions are insufficient. John Wesley, the founder of the Methodist movement, discovered a self-righteous desire to help wasn't enough during his failed missionary work in the American colony of Georgia.

In 1735, with a bagful of good intentions, Wesley attempted to convert to Christianity the Chickasaws who lived near the new town of Savannah. His stiff-necked approach demanding strict adherence to legalism, his all-too-ready criticism of any activity he found distasteful, and his refusal to listen to what the Chickasaws already believed and what their concerns were, led to the complete failure of his "mission amongst the savages."

Anyone who approaches a people with the belief they are "savage" already has lost the opportunity to evangelize effectively. Anyone who won't listen, loses the chance to explain. Wesley's American mission failed with the English Georgia colonists, as well. Again, his inflexibility and his tongue lashings of parishioners not measuring up to his standard of Christianity caused his work to collapse. Wesley left the North American continent a dejected man, a miserable failure despite his good intentions.

In bringing any religious message, we need to remember the teacher's admonition, "A gentle answer turns away wrath, but a harsh word stirs up anger," Proverbs 15:1

Perhaps somewhere at sometime, the in-your-face brand of judgmental Christianity made converts. But that form of evangelism is as outdated and useless as my manual, key-jamming Royal typewriter.

Effective evangelism is like the Internet. It provides information. It listens and answers questions. But more than the Internet, more than old-fashioned preaching, more than any creed, it relies predominantly on one very rarely practiced concept expressed in the writings of almost all the scriptural religions. It is called the Ethic of Reciprocity.

The founder of the Baha'i faith expressed it as, "O son of being! Ascribe not to any soul that which thou wouldst not have ascribed to thee, and say not that which thou doest not," *Hidden Words of Baha'u'llah,* No. 29.

Hinduism, perhaps the oldest continuously practiced faith tradition, says, "This is the sum of duty: Do naught unto others which would cause you pain if done to you," Mahabharata, 5:1517.

Judaism, in contention with Hinduism as the oldest current religion, says, "[L]ove your neighbor as yourself," Leviticus 19:18.

Taoism calls on all moral individuals to "[r]egard your neighbor's gain as your own gain, and your neighbor's loss as your own loss," *T'ai Shang Kan Ying P'ien,* 213-228.

In Islam, the ethic is taught as, "None of you believes until he wishes for his brother what he wishes for himself," *An-Nawawi's Forty Hadiths,* No. 13.

For the Buddhist, it is known as *ahimsa* and states simply, "Hurt not others in ways that you yourself would find hurtful," *Udana-Varga* 5:18.

For the Christian, it is known as the Golden Rule from the Sermon on the Mount: "[D]o to others what you would have them do to you," Matthew 7:12. When we speak about religion, we must evangelize as we want to be evangelized to.

Glossary

Abraham: The patriarch of three monotheistic religions: Judaism, Christianity, and Islam. All three believe Abraham received instruction from God to move around the Fertile Crescent from Ur on the Euphrates River near the Persian Gulf to the Land of Canaan, current-day Israel and the West Bank. Each faith also teaches that Judaism and Christianity descend through Isaac, Abraham's son with his wife Sarah, and Islam teaches it descends through Ishmael, Abraham's son with Sarah's maid, Hagar.

Accident: In ancient Greek thought, all material things were made up of substance and accidents. An accident was what an object looked like, smelled like, felt like, tasted like, sounded like, and so on. Substance was the core quality of the thing.

Affusion: *See* Infusion.

Afterlife: Most religions believe some part of a human being continues after death. Many identify this continuing part as the soul or spirit. There is tremendous divergence on the soul or spirit's environment after physical death.

Age of Accountability: The time in a person's life when she is responsible for her own acts. The age differs, but many religions choose the ages of seven and eight years.

Agnostic: Literally means "no knowledge." An agnostic is a person who says he does not know whether any deity exists or not, because the matter cannot be proven either way.

Ahimsa: The concept a person should do no harm, found in Hinduism, Buddhism, and Jainism.

Anabaptist: Meaning "rebaptizer," the historical group proclaimed infant baptism ineffective and insisted everyone baptized as a child needed to be baptized again. Anabaptists believe a person must be able to express faith in Christ before being baptized.

Apocalypse: Literally means "revelation," but has come to be used to refer to the time when God will win the great battle between good and evil and judge all people.

Apostasy: Often used to mean to extreme heresy, it actually refers to a person publicly denouncing her religion and perhaps going to another.

Apostle: Means "one sent out." In Christianity, an apostle was one of the twelve individuals chosen by Jesus to take his message to the world after his death. Paul, who was not among that group, is often referred to as the Apostle to the Gentiles.

Apostles' Creed: *Creed* comes from a Latin word meaning "belief." A creed is a short statement of a group's core beliefs. The Apostles' Creed is used in the western church but not in the eastern Christian church. It came together in basically its current form in what is today France during the eighth century. Some Protestant groups refuse this and all creeds on the grounds that the Bible is the only creed needed.

Arminianism: Named for Jacobus Arminius, the doctrine Christ died to save all people, not just a few elect individuals.

Aspersion: Generally, a form of baptism in which water is sprinkled on the person being baptized. Specifically, in the Roman Catholic Church, aspersion occurs when the priest sprinkles water on the congregation with an aspergillus—a type of brush—as a means of reminding the flock of their baptisms.

Atheist: Comes from the Greek meaning "no god." Individuals adhering to atheism generally say there is no proof of the existence of any god; therefore, they don't believe in a deity.

Atonement: A penitent act in which a person or community is returned to a proper relationship with God or gods.

Auditor: In Scientology, a person who assists a believer in connecting with his thetan, which may be analogized to the soul in other faiths.

B.C.E.: Abbreviation for "before the common era." It is a calendar term used instead of "B.C.," meaning "before Christ," when discussing the year of an event with individuals who are not Christian.

Bab: Name taken by Syed Ali Muhammad in Persia during 1844 when he founded Babism, precursor to the Baha'i Faith. The Arabic name means "door" or "gate." Before his 1850 execution, the Bab announced God's "Promised One" would soon arrive.

Babylonian Exile: One of the great defining moments of Jewish history. When the Babylonians conquered Jerusalem in 587-86 B.C.E., they removed Israelites from Israel and resettled them in Babylon, a city about fifty miles south of today's Baghdad, Iraq. The exile ended in 536 B.C.E., with the Edict of Cyrus, which freed the Hebrews to return home.

Baha'u'llah: An Arabic name meaning "Glory for God," taken by Mizra Hussein Ali, a Persian nobleman, in 1852 after being exiled to Iraq. He identified himself as the "Promised One of God" predicted by the Bab. Baha'u'llah founded the Baha'i Faith.

Baptism: A ritual in which water is used to purify a believer. Depending on the faith tradition, the act is either merely symbolic or the actual bestowal of forgiveness.

Beatitude: Comes from the Latin for "blessing."

Bible: The name given scriptures used by Jewish and Christian faiths. The Christian Bible consists of the Hebrew Bible and the New Testament. Roman Catholic and Eastern Orthodox churches include additional writings to what they and Protestants call the Old Testament.

Book of Mormon: Scripture revealed to Joseph Smith, founder of the Church of Jesus Christ of Latter-day Saints, used in addition to the Bible. Mormon was one of the leaders of the Nephites and a person chosen to add to the Tablets of Nephi, which eventually become the Book of Mormon.

Brahma: One manifestation of the Hindu Trinity. The godly manifestation of the Supreme Being which is responsible for creation.

Brahman: In Hinduism, the Supreme Being, Primal Soul, and Ultimate Reality. Brahman is recognized as the perfection of being. The name comes from a Sanskrit word meaning "expansion, growth, or manifestation." Also called *Neti-Neti,* meaning "not this, not that." *Brahman* is also the name given the highest Hindu social class. Referring to this caste, the word is also spelled Brahmin.

C.E.: Abbreviation for "common era." It is a calendar term used instead of "A.D.," *anno Domini,* meaning "in the year of the Lord," when discussing the year of an event with individuals who are not Christian.

Caliph: From an Arabic word meaning "successor." The name given Mohammed's successors from the seventh to the thirteenth centuries C.E.

Catechism: Teachings on faith. A written catechism can be extensive, such as the Roman Catholic Catechism, or fairly short such as some of the Greek Orthodox catechisms. Usually presented in a question-and-answer format.

Catholic: Actually means "universal," although many people now use it to refer to the Roman Catholic Church.

Catholic Reformation: Actions taken by the Roman Catholic Church in the late Fifteenth and early Sixteenth centuries to revamp religious orders, increase clerical education, protect doctrine, and change practices. Sometimes called the "Counter-Reformation."

Celestial Kingdom: The highest of three levels of heaven as understood by the Church of Jesus Christ of Latter-day Saints.

Chakra: In yoga, a bodily energy center.

Chi: In Taoism, life-giving energy which consists of yin and yang. *See* yin and yang.

Christ: Comes from the Greek meaning "anointed one." It's the same term as the Hebrew-based *Messiah.* Used to refer to Jesus of Nazareth in both the Christian New Testament and the Muslim Qur'an.

Church: Used various ways. When used in opposition to *denomination,* it means a group of adherents who are following the one true way. It can also mean any group of believers although it is almost exclusively used to refer to Christian congregations.

Companion: The title given individuals who accompanied Mohammed during the early years of Islam. A companion's writings bear greater authority than the words of other Muslims explaining Islam's precepts.

Consecrate: The act of blessing something or someone to set it or her apart for special service.

Consubstantiation: Martin Luther's understanding of what happens when the bread and wine of Holy Communion are consecrated. While the bread and wine retain their qualities, the body and blood of Christ are believed to be in, over, and under them.

Continental Reformation: Commonly referred to as the "Protestant Reformation." The Continental Reformation connotes the changes in Christianity that occurred in parts of continental Europe, starting with Martin Luther's actions in 1517. The English Reformation denotes such changes caused by Parliament and King Henry VIII withdrawing the Church of England from the Roman Catholic Church. Luther's ideology took hold in parts of current-day Germany and Scandinavia. John Calvin's ideology held sway in the present Hungary, Switzerland, the Netherlands, Scotland, and parts of Germany.

Counter-Reformation: *See* Catholic Reformation.

Creator: In philosophical terms, the First Cause that brought the universe into being. In religious terms, this cause is called God or one of many gods.

Cremation: The act of burning a deceased person's body, practiced in Hinduism and other eastern religions and increasingly frequent in the West, especially among Christians.

Crucifixion: Method of execution whereby the condemned individual is nailed or tied to a cross until he dies of dehydration, starvation, exposure, loss of blood, or inability to breathe because of the body's weight constricting the diaphragm and lungs.

Cult: Usually seen as a small group of believers following unorthodox faith practices and guided by a charismatic leader.

Dance: In traditional Native American and traditional African religions, the expression of religious truth through movement. Dance encompasses storytelling as well as thanksgiving, offering, and request.

Deism: The belief God created the universe but allows it to unfold without further divine intervention.

Deity: When capitalized, refers to the one God; when lower-case, refers to gods.

Denomination: A group with identifiable practices and theology within a larger faith tradition. Typically used to classify various Christian groups, although it can also be used when speaking of different sects in other religions. When used in opposition to *church,* it denotes a body that believes it has one correct way but not the only correct way of understanding the divine.

Disciple: Comes from the same Greek word that gives us *discipline.* Technically, a disciple is a student learning about a field of knowledge in an organized manner. Generally, it is used to refer to a follower of a teacher or faith.

Eight-fold Path: *See* Noble Eight-fold Path.

Elect: In predestination, the small group of people chosen by God to be saved at the end of the current era.

Elements: When speaking of Holy Communion, the bread and wine (or grape juice or water) which signify the body and blood of Christ.

Eleusinian Mysteries: A popular ancient Greek cult honoring Demeter and her daughter Persephone, headquartered at Demeter's Temple in Eleusis, near Athens.

E-Meter: Short for "electropsychometer," a device used by the Church of Scientology to help adherents become clear-minded and recover abilities lost because of interference from the world around us.

End Times: The common term used in various religions to describe the time when God will judge all people and restore the God/human relationship believed to have existed at creation. A better term is "end of the era" since each apocalyptic religion foretells a continuing or renewed existence.

English Reformation: Commonly referred to as part of the "Protestant Reformation." The English Reformation connotes the changes in Christianity that occurred in England when King Henry VIII and Parliament (sometimes known as the Reformation Parliament) withdrew the Church of England from communion with the Roman Catholic Church during the 1530s.

Epistle: A letter or similar correspondence, refers to portions of the New Testament originally written as letters to various churches. The epistles include, for example, the books of Jude, James, Romans, and First and Second Corinthians.

Ethic of Reciprocity: The idea found in most religions saying a person must treat others as she wants to be treated herself. In American society, it is often called the Golden Rule.

Ethics: The rules a group adopts as its guide for behavior.

Eucharist: From the Latin term for "thanksgiving." In some churches, it is the name given to Holy Communion.

Evangelical: Usually refers to believing every person has a responsibility to tell others about Jesus Christ.

Evangelize: Comes from one of various Greek words meaning "to proclaim." Means to tell the good news. The good news is the story of Christ.

Evil: Typically used to refer to immoral actions but can also be used to refer to amoral events causing undesired consequences.

Exaltation: In Mormonism, it is the gift of eternal life in God's presence.

Experience: In Methodism, a person's individual contact with the Holy Spirit, in which the Spirit may reveal religious truth.

Faith: Heartfelt set of beliefs concerning the divine.

Four Noble Truths: Basic concepts taught by Siddhartha Gautama, known as the Buddha. They are the Truth of Suffering, which holds life is suffering; Truth of Arising, which teaches suffering arises from craving; Truth of Cessation, which says that craving can be stopped by enlightenment; and Truth of the Path, which says enlightenment is found on the Noble Eight-fold Path. See Noble Eight-fold Path.

Free Will: Humanity's ability to make choices, including the choice to accept or reject God's offer of salvation.

Fruit of the Vine: Used to refer to grapes but most especially wine.

Fruits: A person's accomplishments.

Fundamentalist: Technically a person who accepts all of the Five Fundamentals adopted by the Niagara Bible Conference, specifically (1) the Bible is the inerrant word of God; (2) Jesus is divine; (3) Mary was a virgin when Jesus was born; (4) Christ's sacrifice on the cross provided atonement for human sin; and (5) Jesus was bodily resurrected, ascended, and will return physically to the world.

Gentile: Denotes a non-Jewish person.

Gnostic: From the Greek meaning "knowledge." At the beginning of the Common Era, there were many Gnostic groups in the Mediterranean world. Each believed they possessed secret knowledge about the nature of the universe and human beings.

God: Spiritual being worshipped by various religions. When capitalized, refers to the monotheistic understanding of Supreme Being, First Cause, or Ultimate Reality. Names given God include Allah, Yahweh, and Jehovah. When lower-case, any of multiple spiritual beings who control the world or some aspect of it, such as Zeus, the classical Greeks' chief god; Ra, the ancient Egyptians' sun god; Odin, the Norse chief god, or Quetzalcoatl, the Aztecs' feathered serpent god.

Gospel: Comes from one of various Greek words meaning "good news." Usually applied to the story about Christ, especially the New Testament books of Matthew, Mark, Luke, and John. Has come to mean "truth" in Christian vernacular.

Grace: The unearned gift of forgiveness provided by God, leading to ultimate salvation.

Great Schism: Refers to the division of the Christian Church into the Roman Catholic Church in the West and the Orthodox Church in the East in 1054 C.E.—although some put the date at 1204, when crusaders sacked Constantinople. Also referred to as the East-West Schism to differentiate it from two other events also known as great schisms: the "West Schism," a temporary Roman Catholic split between competing lines of popes in Rome and Avignon, France, and the "Old Believers Schism" protesting Patriarch Nikon's mid-seventeenth century reforms in the Russian Orthodox Church.

Hadith: An Arabic word meaning "tradition." It is a set of writings that tell what Mohammed and his companions did and what they taught.

Hajj: The pilgrimage all physically and financially able Muslims are expected to make to Mecca at least once in a lifetime. It is one of the Five Pillars of Islam. Also spelled *haj* or *hadj.*

Hebrew: Believed to come from an ancient Egyptian term meaning "nomad." Refers both to the people and the language of the land of Israel from ancient days.

Hebrew Bible: Jewish scripture consisting of the Torah, also known as the Pentateuch; the *Neb'im,* translated as "the Prophets"; and the *Ketubim,* translated as "the Writings." The Hebrew names are sometimes condensed to the acronym *Tanakh,* to refer to the entire Hebrew Bible. Altogether, there are thirty-nine books in Hebrew scripture. Occasionally, the books will be counted as thirty-five because of combining such writings as First and Second Kings and Ezra and Nehemiah.

Hedonism: A philosophical system that says comfort and pleasure are the greatest goods.

Heifer: A young female bovine—a cow—that has not given birth.

Heresy: A teaching considered false by religious authorities. Comes from a Greek word meaning "to take to oneself."

Hindu: The name given by westerners to the otherwise unnamed indigenous religion of India, existing for some four thousand years or more, following the Aryan arrival on the Subcontinent. It is marked by extremely wide variations in practices and beliefs, ranging from monotheism to extreme polytheism.

Holy: To be set apart, to be clean, to be pure.

Holy Communion: A ritual in most Christian churches in which the final meal eaten by Jesus Christ is reenacted with bread and wine (or grape juice or water). It signifies Christ's atoning sacrifice on behalf of humankind.

Holy of Holies: See Most Holy Place.

Holy Place: In Judaism, an interior portion of first the Tabernacle, and then the Temple, that was entered only by priests. In Adventism, the site Jesus ascended to in Heaven and which he left later to go the Most Holy Place, a higher level of Heaven.

Honor: To give special deference or recognition to.

Idol: From the Greek for "image." An idol is a representation of a god or spirit. While many of the world's religions approve of idols and use them in worship, monotheistic religions oppose them.

Imam: A Muslim prayer leader. As Islam has moved into the industrialized West, imams have sometimes taken on roles similar to Jewish rabbis, Catholic priests, and Protestant pastors.

Immersion: A form of baptism in which the person being baptized is completely submerged in water. Some groups require three immersions; others, only one.

Inerrancy: Usually part of the phrase "biblical inerrancy." In its most extreme form, it is the belief the Bible contains no errors whatsoever. In a less extreme form, it is the belief the Bible contains no errors on religious matters.

Infusion: A form of baptism in which water is poured over the body or head of the person being baptized. Also known as affusion.

Judgment: In monotheistic religions, God's final determination of which individuals are saved or damned for eternity.

Karma: From the Sanskrit for "action." Typically used to refer to goodness or badness attached to a soul as the result of an action. In Hinduism, the balance of good and bad karma will determine how a person is reincarnated. All acts, regardless of morality, immorality, or amorality have karmic consequences.

Koran: An English spelling of the Muslim holy book. The preferred spelling today is *Qur'an,* as a better approximation of the Arabic word.

Kosher: A Hebrew term meaning "permitted." It is typically applied to dietary practices. Also spelled *kasher.*

Krishna: A god historically understood as an avatar or manifestation of the Hindu god Vishnu. He is considered the incarnation of divine love.

Latter-day Saints: In the New Testament, believers in Christ are referred to as saints. In Mormonism, current believers are contemporary—or "latter-day"—saints. *Latter-day* also connotes the belief that Christ's Second Coming is imminent.

Legalism: Belief that following certain rules will guarantee a person's ultimate salvation.

Lord's Supper: Another name for Holy Communion or the Eucharist, especially popular in non-sacramental Protestant churches. The name recalls the last meal Jesus ate before his betrayal, trial, and crucifixion.

Masoretic Text: The Masoretes were Jewish scholars who made sure copies of the Hebrew Bible were accurate. Their name comes from a Hebrew word meaning "tradition." The document referred to as the Masoretic Text is the Hebrew Bible believed to have been copied by these individuals around 1000 C.E.

Messiah: Comes from the Hebrew meaning "anointed one." It's the same term as the Greek-based *Christ.* Used to refer to Jesus of Nazareth in both the Christian New Testament and the Muslim Qur'an.

Messianic Age: In Judaism, the time when God will send an individual who will redeem or save the Israelite nation and the world. In Christianity, a time that has already come but will arrive again with the second appearance of Christ.

Millennium: Literally one thousand years. In Christianity, the Book of Revelation teaches Christ will rule on earth for one thousand years of peace following his return. Following that time, a great battle will be fought between the forces of good and the forces of evil and eventually won by the good, led by God. Premillennialists believe the time will be a real future event. Postmillennialists see the story as symbolic but with a real time of peace in the future. Amillennialists understand the whole revelation as symbolism referring to a believer's inner peace.

Mishnah: From the Hebrew for "repetition," it is a set of rules written by rabbis in the late second century C.E. for living as a Jewish believer. The rules had previously existed in oral form.

Mitzvah: Hebrew term meaning "commandment." Also used to refer to an act of kindness fulfilling a commandment.

Moeksha: In Hinduism and Jainism, the final release of the soul from the world into a blissful existence. Also spelled *Moksha.*

Monotheist: An individual who believes in only one god.

Mosque: From the Arabic for "place of prostration," the building where Muslims gather for prayer. It usually includes a room for holding shoes which cannot be worn inside; separate places for men and women to wash in preparation for prayer; a large, unadorned room without seating for prayer, and a *minbar,* or raised platform, where the speaker delivers the sermon, known as the *khutbah.*

Most Holy Place: In Adventism, the higher level of Heaven where Jesus went at the beginning of the Millennium. In Judaism, the inner-most room of the Temple or Tabernacle, where the Ark of the Covenant was kept. Entered once a year only by the chief priest. Also known in Judaism as the Holy of Holies.

Muslim: Literally means "one who submits." Spelled with a capital *M,* a Muslim is an adherent of Islam. Spelled with a lower-case *m,* a muslim is a righteous person.

Mysticism: In theistic terms, a way of understanding the divine through direct experience achieved through trance, mediation, prayer, or other means.

New Jerusalem: In the New Testament Book of Revelation, the earthly place of sublime existence where people will live after judgment.

New Testament: The twenty-seven books added to the Bible by Christians, including the Gospels, which tell the story of Christ; Acts, which tells the history of the early church; the epistles, which are letters by Paul, Peter, James, John, Jude and their followers, giving advice to early churches and believers; and Revelation or the Apocalypse, which tells a mystical story about the eventual triumph of God and the forces of good over Satan and the forces of evil.

Nicene Creed: *Creed* comes from a Latin word meaning "belief." A creed is a short statement of a group's core beliefs. The Nicene Creed is used in both the eastern and western Christian churches, although the East rejects an addition used by the West, which says the Holy Spirit proceeds from "the Father and the Son." The East refuses "and the Son" because no church council adopted the amendment. This creed was written by the First Council of Nicaea, called by newly converted Roman Emperor Constantine, in the first half of the fourth century, C.E. Many Protestant groups refuse this and all creeds on the grounds that the Bible is the only creed needed.

Night of Power: The time when God, Allah, began revealing the Qur'an to Mohammed in the Arabian Desert, approximately fifteen hundred years ago.

Ninety-five Theses: A list of grievances Martin Luther wrote and is said to have nailed to the door of the church in Wittenberg, Germany, on October 31, 1517. While the "Ninety-five Theses" concerned many topics, a prevalent issue was the Roman Catholic Church's selling of indulgences. In Luther's time, an indulgence was understood as an act that could help a deceased loved one shorten his time in Purgatory and go on to Heaven.

Nirvana: In Buddhism, the state of human existence following enlightenment, in which the person is released from the cycle of reincarnation. Usually said to be incapable of being described.

Noble Eight-fold Path: In Buddhism the route to enlightenment. The eight parts are right view, or accepting Buddhist teachings; right resolve, which is committing to religious study; right speech, which consists of truth telling and thoughtful speaking; right action, which means abstaining from wrong behavior; right livelihood, which requires an occupation harming no one; right effort, which is control of thoughts; right mindfulness, which means being constantly aware; and right meditation, which is developing calm through special techniques so the mind can be fully awakened.

Old Testament: Based on the Hebrew Bible, the books included in the larger and earlier portion of the Christian Bible. The various Christian churches do not agree on all of the books that are included. Most Protestants use the same material as found in the Hebrew Bible but in a different order. Roman Catholics and Eastern Orthodox include other ancient books, including those found in the Septuagint.

Open Theism: The belief God gives all people free will.

Ordinance: A law or command. In Protestantism, it is often used in opposition to *sacrament*. In that case, an ordinance is a command by God to perform a ritual but the performance does not guarantee salvation or bestow grace.

Orthodox: Literally means "right thought." In Christianity, applied to the branch of Christianity in the eastern Mediterranean which remained after the Great Schism of 1054 C.E., which divided the Christian world, with the Roman Catholic Church in the western Mediterranean. While we typically refer to the Eastern Orthodox, with their Greek, Antiochian, Russian, and other eastern churches, there is also a branch of churches known as the Oriental Orthodox. In Judaism, *Orthodox* is applied to the most conservative school.

Pagan: A term usually applied to indigenous religions that are not monotheistic. It is often considered derogatory but of late has been embraced by certain New Age and Wiccan groups.

Pantheon: The list of gods in polytheistic religions.

Parable: A story told for educational purposes.

Parinirvana: In some forms of Buddhism, Nirvana is understood as enlightenment while an individual remains physically alive, and Parinirvana is the state of the soul following bodily death.

Perdition: Utter damnation.

Personal God: A deity who can be known and who has identifiable characteristics, a being as opposed to a mere force.

Predestination: The doctrine that God has chosen certain souls to be saved at judgment.

Predetermination: The concept God controls everything happening in the universe.

Premortal Life: In Mormonism, the soul's existence prior to birth in a human being.

Protestant: Technically, a person who argued against the Holy Roman Empire's edict preventing regional princes from deciding whether the people in their territory would all follow Catholicism or Luther's reformed church.

Protestant Reformation: See Continental Reformation.

Qur'an: Islam's holy book. In Arabic it means "to recite."

Ramadan: The month in the Islamic calendar preceding the Night of Power. It is a time of fasting from dawn to dusk.

Reincarnation: Belief a soul inhabits various physical bodies throughout time. When one body dies, the soul is placed in a new body.

Repent: To turn away from one way of life and to move toward another, to have a change of heart.

Resurrection: Belief in Islam, Judaism, and Christianity all people will be brought back to physical life for God's final judgment. Also the belief in Christianity the human Jesus Christ was brought back to life after his crucifixion.

Sabbath: The day of rest as commanded by God, a day of worship. In Judaism and some Christian faiths, it is Saturday. There is a difference in the way some groups measure Saturday. Following ancient tradition, the Hebrew faith recognizes a day as beginning at sundown instead of sunrise; therefore, following the civil calendar, the Sabbath is from sundown Friday to sundown Saturday. In most Christian traditions, the Sabbath is Sunday in commemoration of the day Jesus rose from the dead. For Muslims, the day of group worship, though not strictly Sabbath, is Friday. It is understood as the day Adam was created and the day of Allah's coming judgment.

Sacrament: A ritual believed to bestow God's grace on an individual. In the Orthodox and Roman Catholic churches, there are seven sacraments: Baptism, Eucharist, Confirmation or Chrism, Marriage, Reconciliation or Repentance and Confession, Ordination, and Anointing of the Sick or Holy Evchelaion, often known incorrectly as Last Rites. In Protestant churches recognizing sacraments, there are typically two: Baptism and Holy Communion.

Sacrificial Worship: The practice of offering slaughtered animals or other objects to a deity in exchange for the forgiveness of sin or to assure that a god or spirit acts in a certain manner.

Salat: Arabic for "prayer." It is also used to refer to one of the Five Pillars of Islam which requires all Muslims to pray five times a day.

Salvation: Some religions teach both the world and humanity have been corrupted from God's original plan; therefore, each needs to be rescued—or saved—from themselves and horrible approaching consequences not only in this physical life but in the afterlife. The means of providing that rescue and the rescue itself are known as salvation.

Samsara: In Buddhism, the cycle of birth, death, and rebirth, also known as cyclic existence.

Satan: From the Hebrew *ha-satan,* meaning "the adversary." A character in the Book of Job but not otherwise mentioned in the Hebrew Bible. (For example, the serpent in the Garden of Eden is merely a "wily" creature.) Mentioned often in the New Testament as the source of evil.

Saum: Arabic for "fasting."

Saved: *See* salvation.

Scripture: Writings that are given special authority because they are believed to be given by a deity or a holy person acting on behalf of the deity.

Second Coming: The anticipated return of Jesus Christ to earth, setting in motion events leading to the final judgment.

Sect: A group following certain religious practices.

Septuagint: A translation of Hebrew scriptures into Greek, believed compiled in Alexandria, Egypt, sometime between 300 and 200 B.C.E.

Shi'ite: A Muslim within a school of Islam that believes only relatives of Mohammed should have been his successor. Of three major groups in Islam, Shia is the middle in size, although tremendously smaller than the Sunni group.

Shinto: Native Japanese religion which is animistic in form.

Shiva: One of the gods in the Hindu Trinity. Shiva is the destroyer god, who is seen as necessary for ultimate cosmic development. Also transliterated *Siva.*

Shivah: Hebrew for "seven," in Judaism it refers to the seven days of intense mourning following a death.

Substance: The essential nature of a thing. Aristotle considered it something that could exist by itself and which no other thing could also be.

Sufi: A Muslim mystic and the smallest of the three major groups in Islam.

Sunnah: Coming from the Arabic word for "custom," the *Sunnah* consists of writings about the life and sayings of Mohammed.

Sunni: A member of the largest group within Islam. Sunnis comprise about eighty-five percent of Muslims.

Surah: An Arabic term meaning "chapter." It refers to a chapter in the Qur'an.

Synagogue: From the Greek for "assembly," the building where Jews gather for worship. The synagogue as an institution began during the Babylonian Exile. Originally, it was a place for study and then took on social welfare responsibilities. As Hebrews spread throughout the ancient Mediterranean world, the synagogue obtained more significance, and with the destruction of the Temple in 70 C.E., it became the place of communal worship. In Judaism, the home is the major worship site.

Synoptic Gospels: The New Testament books of Matthew, Mark, and Luke. *Synoptic* comes from Greek words meaning "appearing similarly," applied to these books because they tell a very similar story about Jesus, while the Gospel of John offers a unique view of Christ.

Tabernacle: A group of tents constructed by the Israelites for worship in the desert and in Israel until the construction of the First Temple by Solomon.

Telestial Kingdom: The lowest of three levels of heaven as understood by the Church of Jesus Christ of Latter-day Saints.

Temple: A building or other constructed place for worshipping a deity. In Judaism, it referred to the structure in Jerusalem which was the only legal place for sacrifices to be offered. In Reform Judaism, it is often the name given to a place of worship that other forms of Judaism call a synagogue. Reform Judaism understands prayer and other forms of current worship to have replaced ancient sacrifices for all time, thus any place where a congregation of Jews worships may be a temple.

Ten Commandments: Found at Exodus 20:1-17 and Deuteronomy 5:1-21 and also known as the Decalogue. The Ten Commandments comprise the basic law of the Bible, including such requirements as having only one God, resting on the Sabbath, and prohibiting murder, stealing, and other anti-social acts.

Terrestrial Kingdom: The second of three levels of heaven as understood by the Church of Jesus Christ of Latter-day Saints.

Theotokos: Means "God-bearer," and is the term used in Orthodox Christianity, especially the Greek Orthodox Church, to refer to the Virgin Mary.

Thetan: In Scientology, the spiritual core of a human being, capable of continued life without need for a physical body.

Third Temple: A yet-to-be-constructed building some in Judaism see as the future focus of the faith's worship. It would replace the Second Temple which was destroyed by the Romans in 70 C.E. The Second

Temple replaced the First Temple which was destroyed by the Babylonians in 587-86 B.C.E. The First Temple replaced the Tabernacle. *See* Temple and Tabernacle.

Tithe: In Judaism and some Christian churches, the requirement a person give ten percent of her income to God by contributing it to the synagogue or church.

Tradition: Teachings from the early church, especially from councils of church leaders.

Transubstantiation: The view that the bread and wine of Holy Communion are changed into the actual body and blood of Christ when consecrated.

Trefah: A Hebrew term meaning "forbidden." It is applied to foods that are not kosher.

Trinity: In Christianity, the belief the Creator or Father, Son Jesus Christ, and the Holy Spirit or Holy Ghost are three separate persons but one Godhead. In Hinduism, the three gods Brahma, Vishnu, and Shiva, through whom human beings experience the one, true Supreme Being or Reality, Brahman. Hindus accept the Christian Trinity, as well.

Upper Room: The place where Jesus of Nazareth consumed his last meal with his followers. It is also one of the places where the Apostles and others were gathered when the resurrected Jesus came to them.

Venerate: To show great respect.

Vishnu: One of the gods of the Hindu Trinity. Vishnu is the protector of the universe. He is said to have one thousand names used by his avatars. An avatar is a physical manifestation of a god when that deity descends to earth.

Vision: An experience of seeing a deity or spirit or being given divine instruction.

Wake: A vigil originally held the night before a funeral to protect the body before burial. It is popular among Irish Catholics. Usually one day, it sometimes extends over three days.

Westminster Confession of Faith: A statement of religious belief prepared during the English Civil War.

Wiccan: An adherent of Wicca, the re-emergence of ancient European religious beliefs centering on nature worship and magic. Adherents, male and female, are known as witches.

Word: A name given Christ in recognition of God's action in the birth and ministry of Jesus and especially in the atonement which the Messiah's death by crucifixion is said to provide. It comes from the idea God has the power to act by speaking alone, as in creating the universe by saying a phrase.

Words of Institution: The phrases of a prayer spoken to prepare bread and wine (or juice) for Holy Communion. In the United Methodist Church, they are, "On the night in which he was betrayed, Jesus took bread, broke it, gave thanks to you [God] and gave it to his disciples, saying, 'Take, eat, this is my body which is given for you. Do this in remembrance of me.' Likewise after the supper, he took the cup, gave thanks to you and passed it to his disciples, saying, 'Drink from this all of you. This is my blood of the new covenant poured out for you and for many for the forgiveness of sins. As often as you drink it, do it in remembrance of me.'"

Works: In Christian terms, actions portraying faith; however, it is believed a person may not obtain salvation through works since he will never be good enough to merit deliverance.

Yang: In Taoism, the male or sunny portion of life-giving energy, or *chi*, which must be kept in balance with the female portion.

Yin: In Taoism, the female or cool portion of life-giving energy, or *chi*, which must be kept in balance with the male portion.

Zakat: In Islam, the requirement each adult give two-and-one-half percent of his excess wealth to charity. It is one of the Five Pillars of Islam.

Zoraster: Founder of a dualistic religion in the Middle East area today encompassed by Iraq and Iran. Zoroastrianism teaches forces of good and evil will war until a final great battle in which good is expected to prevail. Zoroastrianism was practiced during the Babylonian Exile, and the Israelite community may have been exposed to its teachings. The wise men of the Christmas story are thought to be Zoroastrians.

Scripture Index

Baha'i Scripture

Buddhist Scripture

Hindu Scripture

Upanishads

Veda

Mahabharata

Jewish & Christian Scripture

Ordinary practice is to list biblical scripture in the order the books appear in the Bible; however, Jewish, Catholic, Orthodox, and Protestant Bibles do not agree on the books included and do not present the books they agree on in the same order, so scripture is listed here alphabetically.

Hebrew Bible & Christian Old Testament

Christian New Testament

Additional Mormon Scripture

Book of Mormon

Doctrine & Covenants

Pearl of Great Price

Muslim Scripture

Qur'an

In the body of this book, citations to the Qur'an are given as "Surah x:y" because the chapters are numbered consecutively throughout the scripture. In this index, the name of each surah is given for informational purposes.

Sunnah

Hadith

Tao Scripture

Topic Index

A

B

F

I

P

Q

R

S

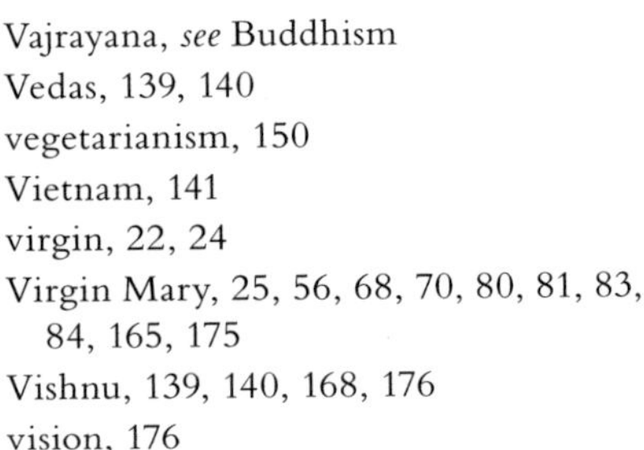

About the Author

Andrew Tevington came to ministry late, following careers in law, politics, and journalism. As a lawyer, he was general counsel to a governor, state assistant attorney general, and assistant district attorney. One of his litigation proficiencies focuses on civil rights cases, including issues of religious freedom. Prior to law school, he was chief legislative aide in Washington, D.C., for a member of the U.S. House of Representatives, press secretary for a U.S. senator, and Oklahoma media consultant for a presidential campaign. As a journalist, he covered sports, police, and city hall before becoming State Capitol bureau chief for a metropolitan newspaper. Throughout this time, Tevington searched for a religious understanding of life. His quest took him through many of the world's religions and gave him the peculiar insight necessary to write this book. Today he serves as local pastor for a United Methodist congregation. He is a graduate of Phillips Theological Seminary, the University of Oklahoma College of Law, and Oklahoma State University's School of Journalism and Broadcasting. He is married to Mary Everest Tevington, an artist. They live in Oklahoma City with two cats.

Send questions about faith traditions to Andrew Tevington at revtev@cox.net or "Our Faiths," 3102 North Classen Boulevard, PMB 125, Oklahoma City, Oklahoma 73118.